GIBSON COUNTY, TENNESSEE

(ILLUSTRATED)

A SERIES OF PEN AND PICTURE SKETCHES

COMPRISING

A PASSING GLANCE AT THE HISTORY, PROGRESS, AND PRESENT STATE OF INDUSTRIAL AND SOCIAL DEVELOPMENT IN GIBSON COUNTY

HISTORICAL, DESCRIPTIVE, AND BIOGRAPHICAL

EDITED AND COMPILED BY W. P. GREENE

Southern Historical Press, Inc.
Greenville, South Carolina

This volume was reproduced from
An 1901 edition located in the
Publisher's private Library

All rights reserved. No part of this publication may be reproduced,
stored in a retrieval system, transmitted in any form, posted
on to the web in any form or by any means without
the prior written permission of the publisher.

Please direct all correspondence and orders to:

www.southernhistoricalpress.com
or
**SOUTHERN HISTORICAL PRESS, Inc.
PO Box 1267
375 West Broad Street
Greenville, SC   29601**
southernhistoricalpress@gmail.com

Originally published: Nashville, TN, 1901
ISBN #0-89308-882-X
All rights Reserved.
Printed in the United States of America

PREFACE.

This little work is discursive rather than exhaustive. It contains some historical, some descriptive, and some biographical matter, but makes no pretense as to detail in regard to any of the subjects treated. Those who expect to find something here about everything and everybody in Gibson County will be disappointed. It is only a series of pen and picture sketches, exhibiting the salient points in the county's industrial and social development, together with a glance at its history and progress. With this exegesis of its scope and purpose, I present it to the public. The work is in some respects a public enterprise, in that it advertises the county abroad and memorializes it at home, thus entitling it to the favor of the wide-awake, progressive people of the county.

I am under obligations to a number of good people for timely and valuable aid in preparing the work. I mention J. H. Koffman, Esq., and his accomplished wife, Mrs. Mattie Boyd Koffman, who assisted me greatly in my sketch work. Mr. James R. Deason, of the law firm of Deason, Rankin and Elder, also gave me great assistance and encouragement.

To Mr. E. E. Benton, of the Herald-Democrat, I am indebted for special courtesies, and to the press of the county in general I owe thanks for editorial favors. Indeed, I may say, I am indebted to all the people of the county with whom I came in contact for courtesies extended and kindly interest in my work.

W. P. GREENE.

REGIONAL HISTORY.

TRACING THE SOVEREIGNTY OF THE COUNTRY.

For the purposes of a work historical and descriptive of Gibson County, Tenn., we are not particularly concerned with the voyages of the Northmen to the Western world, said to have occurred in the year 874; nor with the visit Leif the Lucky, son of Eric the Red, is said to have paid to the coast of North America in the year 1900. If Leif did visit our Eastern coast away back there, five hundred years before Christopher Columbus or Amerigo Vespucci found it, he deserved to lose his sobriquet, "Lucky," for he missed a good thing in not staying with his discovery. Still, we are somewhat interested in the discovery of America, for the reason that if America had not been discovered, Gibson County would have remained terra incognita.

In order to be logical, therefore, we begin the history of Gibson County with some remarks about the discovery of America. It is nothing more than right that the people of Gibson County should know the facts about this event, as two or three very worthy persons have not received the credit they deserved in the matter.

Christopher Columbus got the sole credit

VIEW IN TRENTON, THE COUNTY SEAT, ON A FIRST MONDAY.

for discovering America, though he really did not do it; he only discovered some of the islands adjacent. He never saw the continent of North America; in fact, he died ignorant of the fact that America was a continent at all, and in the full belief that the islands he had discovered were a part of Asia. In consequence of this belief, he called the natives of the islands "Indians," by which name all the natives of both North and South America came afterwards to be designated. Although it is said that there is nothing in a name—which may be true outside of banking circles—yet this was clearly a misnomer and an injustice to the inhabitant of India, who was a decent, civilized individual, compared with the cruel, skulking, treacherous, scalp-taking sans-culottes that prowled in the forests of North America. Another misnomer grew out of this same error of Columbus. The islands were called the "West Indies," perhaps as a kind of protest against the fact that they proved not to be the East Indies, as Columbus had supposed.

Still, we must give Columbus the credit for breaking the ice, as it were, in introducing the old world to the new. Columbus made his discovery of the islands off the coast of America on October 12, 1492. He made three other voyages, the last of which was in 1502, always seeking a passage to India and never reaching America.

The news of Columbus' discovery reached Europe, however, and excited the spirit of adventure and cupidity too, no doubt, among the nations of Western Europe. It must be remembered that with these nations, at this time, India was the land of gold and precious stones and all manner of riches; hence the craze to find a Western passage to India.

Portugal sent out an expedition in 1497, under an experienced navigator, named "Vas-

RESIDENCE OF GEN. W. W. WADE, ATTORNEY-GENERAL OF THE EIGHTEENTH JUDICIAL CIRCUIT.

co da Gama," which actually sailed around the new world on the south and reached India, returning two years later, laden with riches. Da Gama must have seen South America, but we have no record of his landing upon it, nor whether he, like Columbus, thought it a large island lying east of Asia.

Henry VII., of England, sent out an expedition under John and Sebastian Cabot in 1497. They must have sailed in different vessels, as John Cabot reached the northern part of North America in the same year, and named the land he saw "New Found Land;" while Sebastian's voyage did not take place till 1498, when he sailed along the Atlantic Coast as far as the Carolinas and claimed the whole country for England.

I am inclined to think that the Cabots were not Englishmen, as the name has not an English sound, and I have never met with the name in English history or literature. I am inclined to believe that they were Portuguese sailors, employed by King Henry, of England, on account of their experience as navigators. At any rate, this English expedition was the first to discover the mainland of North America, and John and Sebastian Cabot should receive whatever of credit is due therefor.

Whether these navigators were possessed with the current delusion that the land they discovered was a part of Asia, is not known; but it is quite likely they were, as that seems to have been the prevailing belief.

There was an Italian, by name "Amerigo Vespucci," who got a great and lasting honor out of the discovery of the new world, to which he was not entitled. The circumstances which brought this about serve to illustrate the value of advertising and the power of the press. He sailed along the coast of South America in 1506, ten years after da Gama sailed along the same coast and nine years after Sebastian Cabot sailed along the coast of the Carolinas, but he wrote out and published an account of the new land and what he had seen. This account got into the hands of a Dutchman, named "Waldseemüller," who published, in 1507, a geographical work in which he gave the name "America" to the new world. The Italian's name has stuck to the country ever since; and, what is more, this Italian, obscure, except for this, and known nowhere else in history, has thus unwittingly conferred his name upon a nation which, in its own estimation, at least, is the very salt of the earth among nations and divinely appointed to take care of the balance of mankind. It is hoped it will be true to its mission.

The early voyages that succeeded the discovery of Columbus were made partly to see what was to be seen, but mostly in search of gold or other treasure.

MARBLE WORKS OF JAMES GILLEN, HUMBOLDT, TENN.

No attempt was made by any of the nations of Europe to establish homes for their people in the new world. Silence and mystery continued to reign beyond the dark forests that curtained the land, and the muse of history held her pen for a hundred years, waiting to begin the marvelous story of the amalgamation of peoples and the building of a new nation.

It is not my purpose to enter into an account of the explorations and settlements that were begun by the various nations of Europe on the continent of North America at the end of the sixteenth century and in the beginning of the seventeenth century. I shall only briefly outline the history of the settlement, by our English ancestors, of the particular region which embraced the State of Tennessee and the section which forms the subject of these sketches.

My design in this outline is to note specially those controlling acts and events which finally established the sovereignty of the United States of America over the region and led up to the division of the country into States and counties and the formation of local governments.

In the year 1600 almost nothing was known of the interior of North America. It was only known as a vast continent of indefinite extent and proportions, and wondrously endowed by nature with every element necessary to the human race. The fact that it was already occupied by human beings seems to have received but little consideration at the hands of our forefathers. John and Sebastian Cabot had sailed along the Atlantic coast and claimed the land for England by right of discovery, and England proceeded to exercise the rights of ownership thus conferred by granting the land to her subjects. It is to these grants that we must look in tracing our civil divisions and our titles to the lands we occupy, because they have been recognized through all the mutations of time and events as delineating the rights of States and the limits of sovereign proprietorship over the country.

The first permanent settlement that was made by our English ancestors was in the year 1607, at Jamestown, forty miles up the James River. Some previous attempts at settlement had failed. The settlement at Jamestown was by a company called the "Virginia Company" or "London Company." This company received from James I., who was then king of England, a grant of territory which embraced the Atlantic Coast from the thirty-fourth to the thirty-eighth degree of north latitude, and an indefinite extent of country in the interior, presumably as far as the country extended. This grant was extended, two years later, and made to embrace more of the coast; but in 1624, after King James' death, the grants to the London Company were annulled by King Charles I., who took the government of the colony into his own hands, and after that Virginia was a royal province.

The Virginia colonists had a hard time of it for the first ten or twelve years to even preserve their existence; but English tenacity and perseverance eventually triumphed over all obstacles, and the English people became fixed in America.

This was the period when Capt. John Smith, Powhatan, and Pocahontas figured in history. During the next forty years the colonists, with other emigrants from Europe, including some of those grand people, the Huguenots, fleeing from religious persecution in France, spread over the country southward and gave occasion for the establishment of another colonial government.

So, in 1663, King Charles II. executed a most munificent grant, conveying to certain nobles of his court the right to occupy, possess, and govern, subject to the laws of England, all that portion of America lying between the thirty-first and thirty-sixth degrees of north latitude, on the Atlantic Coast, and as far westward as the South Seas. The recipients of this charter were Edward Clarendon, George Albemarle, William Craven, John Berkeley, Anthony Ashley, George Carteret, John Colleton, and William Berkeley.

This grant, and a supplemental grant two years later, extending its northern limit to 36° 30′ north latitude, constituted the title under which North Carolina afterwards claimed and obtained the sovereignty of the region which includes the State of Tennessee. The region covered by this grant was called "Carolina" in honor of King Charles, and continued under the government of North Carolina as colony and State for one hundred and twenty-six years.

In the meantime a settlement was made at the mouth of the Ashley River and named

"Charles Town," and the two portions of the country became designated as "North Carolina" and "South Carolina."

In the year 1729 King Charles divided the country into two provinces, establishing different governments in each. In this division South Carolina was left with the territory above the thirty-first degree of north latitude as far as the Cape Fear River and westward; but afterwards, in 1732, a grant was made to James Edward Oglethorpe by King George, who succeeded King Charles, of the country between the Savannah River and the Alabama River, leaving to South Carolina only that portion east of the Savannah River and an indefinite strip westward.

No royal grant was ever made to any of the country lying west of North Carolina, so that King Charles' grant of 1663 and its enlargement two years after stood as the muniment of title which North Carolina held to all the country west, not assigned to South Carolina nor included in King George's grant to Oglethorpe.

There is a little confusion as to the exact date of this grant of Charles II. to Clarendon and his associates. The histories and encyclopedias which I have consulted place it in the year 1663; Whitney, in his "Land Laws of Tennessee," recites the document itself, which gives the date of its execution as June 30, in the seventeenth year of the reign of Charles II. If we ignore the eleven years of the Commonwealth, or Protectorate, and place the beginning of the reign of Charles II. at the date of his father's death, in 1649, the seventeenth year of his reign would be the year 1666. If we count from the time of his actual accedence to the throne of England, in 1660, the seventeenth year of his reign would be the year 1677. I leave this matter to be straightened out by those who have leisure and taste for the inquiry.

The creation of the royal province of South Carolina, and the grant to Oglethorpe, left to North Carolina all the territory westward between the thirty-fifth degree of north latitude and Virginia. The northern boundary of this territory between North Carolina and Virginia remained unsettled until after the Revolutionary War, when it was finally surveyed and fixed upon the line of 36° 30' north latitude, the present northern boundary of the State of Tennessee.

SOME OF THE MAGISTRATES OF THE COUNTY.

From this time forward the territory of North Carolina remained as delineated by the great grant of Charles II. No king of England changed her boundaries, no other colony disputed her title; her western frontier still extended to the South Seas, and her people remained ignorant of the vastness of her possessions.

England was one hundred and sixty-six years in establishing her title to the countries of America which she claimed by virtue of the discoveries of John and Sebastian Cabot.

From the first settlement at Jamestown in 1607 to the peace of Paris in 1763, England and her colonies were engaged in almost ceaseless war, either with France, Spain, or the Indian tribes, for the possession of the country. Her greatest and bloodiest wars were with the French and the Indians. The French claimed the country about the Great Lakes by right of discovery, and had pushed their explorations and discoveries down the Mississippi River and laid claim to all the country west of the Alleghany Mountains, and pretty much all the continent, except the narrow strip on the Atlantic Coast occupied by the English. This our forefathers would not permit; so a great struggle took place, which resulted in the French being entirely driven from America. The struggle ended in 1763. A treaty was made in that year, to which England, France, and Spain were parties, in which France gave up to England all her claims to the country east of the Mississippi River. In the same treaty France turned over to Spain the city of New Orleans and all of the country west of the Mississippi River, which she had named "Louisiana;" and Spain was also confirmed in her possession of Florida. I will state in passing, for the benefit of casual readers, that Spain afterwards ceded the country west of the Mississippi River back to France, and France sold the same to the United States in 1803. Spain retained Florida until 1819, when she also sold out to the United States.

The treaty of Paris in 1763, fixing the western boundary of England's possessions in the new world, also determined the western limit of North Carolina's holding under her grant from King Charles. The Mississippi River became the South Seas of that instrument.

In the long war that finally established English sovereignty over the disputed portions of North America, the colonists had borne the brunt of the struggle. Their privations and struggles, both in establishing their homes and defending them, had developed in them a spirit of independence and self-confidence that soon brought them into collision with the English Government; and within thirteen years after the treaty of 1763, we find them declaring themselves free and independent, and capable of managing their own affairs.

The descendants of the old North Carolina revolutionists, who form so large a portion of the population of Gibson County, may be proud of the part the old mother State took in asserting and maintaining the rights of freemen in 1776.

In the excitement of impending revolution, North Carolina did not forget her grant from King Charles II. On the eve of confederation with the other colonies to assert and maintain the liberties of all, she passed an Act asserting and declaring her sovereign right to the country embraced in that grant. This Act was passed by the Assembly of North Carolina in 1776.

In 1777 the Assembly erected the whole of the territory west of the mountains into a county of North Carolina and called it "Washington County." This included all of Tennessee.

In 1779 Sullivan County was created out of the northeast corner of the county of Washington.

These were the last acts of sovereign authority exercised by North Carolina over her territory until after the close of the Revolutionary War.

In 1783 the colonies had fought to a triumphant conclusion their war for independence; and England at the treaty of Paris, February, 1783, had acknowledged the independence of each of the American colonies. The form of this acknowledgment was such that it left each of the colonies the sovereignty of the lands it had formerly held by grant from England.

In 1783 the Assembly of North Carolina recommenced the work of dividing its territory into civil divisions, and divided Washington County, designating a small portion south of Sullivan County as "Washington County" and naming the remaining portion "Greene County."

In the same year Davidson County was created on the north line of the territory west of Cumberland Gap.

In 1786 Sumner County was cut off of the east end of Davidson County.

formal Act, she ceded to the United States all the territory she possessed beyond her own limits. For seven years this territory remained the common property of all the people of the United States, open to settlement under the laws provided by the United States for the government of its common territory, except the lands reserved to the Indians and grants previously made by North Carolina.

In 1796 Tennessee was admitted to the Union of States, thus completing the establishment of civil government over all the country embraced in the original grant of lands to North Carolina.

RESIDENCE OF COL. C. H. FERRELL, PRESIDENT MERCHANTS' STATE BANK, HUMBOLDT.

In 1788 Davidson County was again divided, and Tennessee County was created out of its western part.

These were the final acts of sovereignty exercised by North Carolina over the territory she held by virtue of her grant of 1663. None of these acts affected, except by implication, the section in which Gibson County lies.

In 1789 North Carolina ratified and signed the Constitution of the United States and became one of the States of the American Union. In December of the same year, by

The last Act of North Carolina before the cession of her territory to the United States was the creation of Tennessee County off the west end of Davidson County. The Government of Tennessee now took up the work of dividing the territory where North Carolina left off.

In 1796 Tennessee County was divided into two counties—Robertson and Montgomery—and ceased to exist, the name "Tennessee" having been given to the State. Robertson County was created out of the eastern portion, and Montgomery County was left to embrace the remainder, which was all of the western part of the territory.

In 1803 Montgomery County was divided by a line beginning on the Kentucky line thirteen miles west of the meridian of Clarksville and running south to the southern boundary of the State. All west of this line was named "Stewart County." Stewart County thus embraced all of West Tennessee, and, after the Chickasaw Purchase and before the formation of the new counties in West Tennessee, had jurisdiction over all the territory west of the Tennessee River; but Stewart County stood as embracing all of West Tennessee from 1803 to 1818.

I have not space to go into a discussion of the methods adopted by our English ancestors in their dealings with the Indians whom they found in possession of the country. I have an idea that the Indian did not receive the full measure of justice to which he was entitled as the man in possession; still, he was making mighty slow progress in civilization, and required to be hurried up or suppressed. He had no business to be just roaming around, hunting and fishing, and tomahawking and scalping people. It was his duty to go to work, or stand aside and let somebody else do it. He was occupying a pretty large extent of the universe to very little purpose, and it was his duty to divide up with fellows who had been a little crowded in their former habitations. So the exercise of a little compulsion and of a little superior trading talent, on the part of our forefathers, was perhaps justifiable, all things considered.

After the sovereignty of the entire country passed from England to the United States, the rights of the Indian in the soil received greater consideration. He was kept moving, however, but for a consideration—nominal, merely, it is true, but sufficient to give the transaction an air of fairness and open dealing.

As regards our Gibson County region, it was the home and the hunting ground of the Chickasaw tribe of Indians, and was so recognized by the Government of the United States. All of the State of Tennessee west of the Tennessee River was recognized and treated as the hunting ground of this tribe of Indians. No whites were permitted to acquire title to any of its lands. They were

RESIDENCE OF J. FREED, PROMINENT MERCHANT OF TRENTON.

permitted to trade with the Indians and live among them, if they so desired; but the lands continued to remain the public domain of the United States, subject to the Indian right of occupancy. North Carolina had made some grants of land within the territory, but even these were subject to the Indian title. There were a number of these grants in Gibson County. A portion of the land upon which Trenton stands was one of these grants; nearly all the land in the Twenty-fourth District was covered by one of these North Carolina grants.

After the cession of the territory by North Carolina to the general government, in 1789, all grants of lands west of the Tennessee River ceased, and for a period of twenty-nine years West Tennessee continued to be the home and habitat of the Chickasaw tribe of Indians. From all I can gather about the Chickasaw Indians, they seem to have been the most peaceable and least bloodthirsty of any of the tribes that inhabited our Southern country. Their friendship for the whites was very marked through all the bloody wars that attended the settlement of the country; and they seem to have been a tractable and docile people, indisposed to war and inclined to domestication.

On October 19, 1818, at the Treaty Ground, on the Tennessee River, near where Riverton now stands, a great convention took place between the chiefs and head men of the Chickasaw tribe of Indians, on the one side, and Andrew Jackson and Isaac Shelby, commissioners of the United States, on the other.

At this convention the great and final treaty was negotiated, signed, and published, by which the Chickasaw Indians, in consideration of twenty thousand dollars to be paid annually for fifteen years, gave up to the United States all claim, right, and title to the lands lying north of the thirty-fifth parallel, and bounded on the north, east, and west by the Ohio, Tennessee, and Mississippi Rivers. The treaty reads: " Beginning where the thir-

RESIDENCE OF H. M. ELDER, CASHIER GIBSON COUNTY BANK, TRENTON.

ty-fifth parallel cuts across the Tennessee River; west with the parallel to the Mississippi River; up the Mississippi River to the mouth of the Ohio River; up the Ohio River to the mouth of the Tennessee River; up the Tennessee River to the place of beginning." Thus was settled forever the title to the soil of West Tennessee, and thus were opened up the lands to the occupancy and settlement of the white people.

In the year following the treaty a good many white people settled in the region, who, together with those already there, formed the nucleus of population in several parts of the territory.

The State of Tennessee now began the establishing of local civil government throughout the region, and to this end began the dividing up of the country into counties.

On November 19, 1819, Shelby County was delineated and organized. This was the first county created in West Tennessee; others followed, until in a few years the entire region that had been occupied by the Chickasaw Indians was divided into counties, and organized local governments were established over the entire country.

The history of a people passing from the first rude stage of social and industrial life (incident to the occupancy of a new and uninhabited country) to a condition of thorough political, social, and industrial organization is always an interesting and pleasing study. All our American communities have such a history, and it is this fact which gives to American history its peculiar charm and to the American people their peculiar character of independence, resourcefulness, and push that distinguishes them from all the other people of the world.

In many parts of our country the page of history as regards the triumphs of the people over natural forces has closed; in other and newer sections the struggle is still going on. New settlements are being formed, privations endured, and social conveniences and organizations introduced.

Every foot of territory gained in the new world, every advance made in the establishment of social order and the securing of domestic comforts and conveniences, and, indeed, in the establishment of civil government, has been fought for. From the time when the first colonists set foot on American soil down to the present time, the history of the American people has been that of aggressiveness—of warfare upon the forces, moral and physical, that stood in the way of their progress.

GIBSON COUNTY.

ORGANIZATION.

Gibson County was the twelfth county organized in West Tennessee after the Chickasaw Purchase. The words of its institution are as follows:

"AN ACT TO ESTABLISH A NEW COUNTY, WEST OF CARROLL COUNTY, PASSED ON OCTOBER 21, 1823.

"*Be it enacted by the General Assembly of the State of Tennessee*, That a new county, to be called by the name 'Gibson County,' in honor of and to perpetuate the memory of Col. John H. Gibson, shall be, and is hereby, established west of Carroll County; beginning at the northwest corner of Carroll County, running thence west on the fourth sectional line to a point four miles west of the second range line in the Thirteenth District; thence north to the fifth sectional line; thence west on said sectional line to the fifth range line; thence south with the said range line to a point two and one-half miles south of the line separating the Tenth and Thirteenth Districts; thence east parallel with said line to a point directly south of the southwest corner of Carroll County; thence north to the beginning."

Col. John H. Gibson, for whom the county was named, was one of that noble band of pioneers and patriots conspicuous in American history as leaders in the great struggle to establish the supremacy of the American people on the soil of America. He was with Jackson at New Orleans, and during the War of 1812 was in the same command with Dyer, Williamson, Lauderdale, and Elliott. He also served under Wayne in his Northwestern campaign against the Indians. He died in 1823, near Jackson, Tenn., and was there buried with the honors of war. The Legislature of Tennessee, shortly before the Civil War, passed an Act authorizing the removal of his body to the State capital, but his grave could not be identified. Thus this distinguished soldier and patriot sleeps in an unknown grave in the land he loved and served, and hard by the grand county that perpetuates his name and memory.

There are a number of the descendants of Colonel Gibson in the South. He was married to Miss Anna McConn, of Frankfort, Ky., and had three sons and five daughters. One of his grandsons, Capt. Paul Shirley, is in the United States Navy. A granddaughter of his, Miss Frank Dobbs—to whom I am indebted for the above facts about her grandfather—resides at Fort Payne, Ala. Mr. Gibson, of near Rutherford, is also a grandson of Colonel Gibson, and the only one of his descendants living in Gibson County.

In 1870 the boundaries of Gibson County as defined by the Act of its creation were changed somewhat. About thirty square miles of its territory in the southwest corner were taken, which, with other territory taken from Madison, Haywood, and Dyer Counties, was erected into a new county, called "Crockett County," in memory of the famous hunter, statesman, and Texas martyr, David Crockett. Another change was made in the northeast boundary of the county, making the South Fork of the Obion River the dividing line between Gibson County and Weakley County, instead of the fourth sectional line, as provided in the Act of creation. Except these changes, the county remains as first delineated by its organic Act.

If you will look at a good map of Tennessee, you will see that Gibson County is situated near the center of what is denominated "West Tennessee," being that portion of the State lying between the Tennessee River and the Mississippi River; in fact, the exact geographical center of West Tennessee is a few hundred yards south of the southern line of the county.

Speaking generally of West Tennessee, there is probably no other portion of the United States of equal extent that is better fitted by nature for the pursuits of agriculture. Nature has provided every essential here for the hand and home of the tiller of the soil. The soil is fertile and easily tilled; the climate is mild, healthful, and adapted to the growth of every product of the temperate zone; exhaustless veins of limpid water course their way within easy reach beneath the soil; noble forests of timber provide the material for homes and shelter for both man and brute. What more does a country lack that possesses these? I think,

RESIDENCE OF DR. W. F. MATHEWS, BRAZIL.

nothing, except God's blessing upon the work of human hands.

These words in regard to the general section will apply with equal, if not stronger, force to Gibson County. Taken as a whole, there is no other county in West Tennessee richer in natural endowment than Gibson; and as respects the extent of its population and of its agricultural development, it is the leading county in the section, outside of Shelby, and it is second to Shelby only in the number of its population.

There were but few settlers within the limits of Gibson County before its organization. In 1819, so far as I can find any accurate record, there were but three. These were Thomas Fite, John Spencer, and James T. Randolph. In that year Luke Biggs settled

RESIDENCE OF DR. T. J. HAPPEL, NOTED PHYSICIAN AND SURGEON OF THE COUNTY, AND PRESIDENT OF THE COUNTY BOARD OF HEALTH.

about four miles west of where Trenton now stands, and John Eubanks settled near the present site of Bell's Chapel.

In 1822 there were six families in the county. These were the families of Thomas Fite, Isaac Sellers, Luke Biggs, and John Eubanks, on the west side; Oliver Blakemore and James Blakemore, on the east side. David Crockett became a citizen of the region in 1822, settling a little east of where the town of Rutherford now stands.

In 1822 and 1823 settlers entered the county rapidly from Middle Tennessee, East Tennessee, and North Carolina; so that early in 1824, when the county government was inaugurated, the county had a considerable population. As evidence that North Carolina contributed most to the settlement of Gibson County, by far the larger portion of the population of the county to-day is composed of the descendants of North Carolina ancestors. At the time of the organization of the county there were probably within its limits five hundred persons.

The session of the Legislature of 1823 and 1824 sat at Murfreesboro. This Legislature created seven new counties in West Tennessee—McNairy, October 8; Hardeman and Haywood, October 10; Dyer, October 16; Gibson, October 21; Obion, October 24; Tipton, October 27. Provision was made for a local government in each of the counties.

Gibson County was divided into four districts—the Northern, Southwestern, Central, and Southeastern.

The Ninth Judicial Circuit was formed, embracing Gibson County; and John C. Hamilton was elected by the Legislature as judge of the circuit. His commission, from Gov. William Carroll, was issued on and dated October 23, 1823. The Ninth Judicial Circuit, when first created, was composed of the counties of Carroll, Henry, Henderson, Perry, and all the counties to be established west of Carroll and Henry Counties. This brought Gibson County into Judge Hamilton's circuit.

The justices of the peace for Gibson County, elected by the Legislature and commissioned by Governor Carroll, were: William P. Seat, Robert Edmonson, Oliver Blakemore, Benjamin White, Robert Reed, Yarnell Reese, Abner Burgan, John D. Love, William W. Craig, William Killingsworth, and Isham F. Davis.

A commission—composed of James Fentress, Robert Jetton, Benjamin Reynolds, and William Martin—was appointed with instructions to obtain, by purchase or donation, a tract of land of not less than fifty acres, as near the center of the new county as practicable, upon which to locate the county capital.

The first movement in the organization of the county took place at the house of Luke Biggs, about four miles west of the present county seat, on January 5, 1824. On that day the justices of the peace, who had been commissioned by the Governor in pursuance of the Act of the Legislature, met and organized the County Court, or "Court of Pleas and Sessions," as it was then designated. The house in which they met is no longer standing, having given place to a more modern edifice; but the site, as well as the farm, which the event thus made historic, is still in the hands and occupancy of the descendants of Luke Biggs. It is owned by Rev. S. B. Scott, who married a daughter of this pioneer settler of Gibson County.

The Court of Pleas and Sessions was organized by the election of William P. Seat as chairman and Thomas Fite as clerk.

John W. Needham was chosen sheriff; Robert Reed, trustee; William W. Craig, register; and William D. Blakemore, ranger.

I notice that this initial County Court appointed two of its members—Robert Reed and William W. Craig—to the two best offices in the county. This augurs well for the economic talent of that body, and proves that our ancestors were fully alive to the advantages of opportunity.

"Make hay while the sun shines," is a maxim that, I think, was evolved from American experience; at least, it is a maxim that describes with accuracy a trait of the American people. It embodies the very essence of wisdom, and is so universally applicable in all the affairs of life that he who neglects to heed its teachings is pretty apt to fail of a harvest. The sun of official position had begun to shine in Gibson County, and our ancestors of blessed memory proceeded to take advantage of its haymaking energies.

Lack of space will preclude a detailed account of the proceedings of the County Court after its first organization; in fact, such account would be foreign to the design of this publication and prove dull reading for the busy, practical generation of the present day, whose thoughts and energies are more concerned with the present and future than with the musty records of the past. Those, however, who have taste and leisure for such inquiry are referred to my chapter entitled "Incidents of the Early Settlement of Gibson County."

At this time Gibson County was only a wilderness. The face of the country was covered by an almost unbroken forest. As yet, no mill wheels disturbed the silent flow of the rivers; the smoke of the settler's hastily and rudely constructed cabin curled lonesomely among the tree tops, and the small clearings before his door were scarcely large enough to receive the welcoming smile of the

RESIDENCE OF J. W. JETTON, TRENTON.

noonday sun; wild animals lurked in the dark recesses of the forest; and deadly fevers stretched forth their burning hands from the tangled canebrakes. But the sturdy settlers of these untamed wilds heeded not these things; or if they heeded them, with the inherited pluck of their ancestors they attacked them and subdued them. With ax and rifle and a courage and perseverance that nothing could daunt, they hewed and fought their way, until mansions stood where once the lowly cabin had crouched beneath the trees, and billowy fields of cotton and grain spread their broad acres over the spot where the wild beast had made his lair.

The Court of Pleas and Sessions held but one term at the house of Luke Biggs. It held its April term at the house of William C. Love, who lived about four and one-half miles east of the present county seat. From this time forward until the county seat was located, the house of William C. Love was the de facto seat of justice of the county. Here, on May 24, 1824, Judge John C. Hamilton held the first term of the Circuit Court for Gibson County. Joseph H. Talbot was appointed clerk.

The grand jury of this first Circuit Court was composed of the following citizens: William B. G. Killingsworth, foreman; Robert Reed, Isham F. Davis, George F. Crafton, William McKendrick, William W. Craig, Robert Temple, Robert Edmonson, John Spencer, Benjamin White, William Blakemore, Andrew Cole, and John Parker. James R. Chalmers was attorney-general at this time.

During the summer of 1824, the commissioners who had been appointed by the Legislature to select a site for the seat of justice of the county, made choice of a spot near the center of the county, on the North Fork of the Forked Deer River, on which Thomas F. Gibson had built a storehouse and was engaged in selling goods to the settlers. The settlers had given the place the name "Gibsonport." The land belonged to John B. Hogg, James

RESIDENCE OF HON. J. C. M'DEARMON, TRENTON.

Whitaker, Jesse Blackfin, James Caruthers, and Frank McGavock. Hogg and Whitaker donated twenty acres, and the others together donated thirty-six and a quarter acres, making in the aggregate fifty acres for the county seat site, as required by the instructions to the commissioners, and an additional six and a quarter acres, which was set apart as a town common.

At the October (1824) term of the County Court, held at the home of William C. Love, the following commissioners were appointed to lay off the county town of Gibson County: John W. Evans, John W. Buckner, William C. Love, Robert Tinkle, and John P. Thomas.

At the January (1825) term of the court, held at the same place, Robert Jetton, James Fentress, Benjamin Reynolds, and William Martin were allowed one hundred and twelve dollars for their services in locating the county seat. At this term the commissioners who had been appointed at the previous term to lay off the county town were ordered to construct a temporary courthouse in the town of Gibsonport, for the use of the courts of the county, and have the same ready for the use of this court at its next term. The order stipulated that the house should be constructed of hewn logs, one story in height, with a clapboard roof, and floor of rough plank securely pinned down. The dimensions of the house were to be 20x35 feet. A jury room, 10x20 feet in size, was to be made in one end by running a log partition across the building. A convenient bench was to be provided for the use of the court, and such other benches and bar as the commissioners might direct. This rude structure served as the temple of justice of Gibson County until 1829, when it was removed and a two-story brick building erected in its place.

The town commissioners were prompt in the execution of the order of court, and the April (1825) term of the County Court was held in the courthouse in Gibsonport.

Two terms of the Circuit Court were held at the house of William C. Love—its first term on May 24, 1824; its second term on November 25 of the same year. The May (1825) term was held at the courthouse in Gibsonport. The County Court held five of its sessions at the house of William C. Love before the county government became finally settled in a home of its own.

"Gibsonport" continued to be the name of the county seat until February, 1826, when an Act of the Legislature confirming the acts of the commissioners in locating the county seat gave it the name "Trenton."

GROWTH AND DEVELOPMENT OF THE COUNTY.

The influx of population into the new county was rapid. Settlers from Middle Tennessee, East Tennessee, North Carolina, and Virginia spread themselves over the county, and soon the county was dotted with settlements and incipient plantations. Roads were opened through the forests, mills were erected upon the streams, stores were set up here and there; and within a very short time after the county was organized, a fair degree of social order had been attained, and many social conveniences had been established. Still, everything was rude and of hasty contrivance—from the log courthouse in the county town to the most pretentious residence of the wealthiest citizen.

The County Court, at its April (1824) term, ordered a road to be opened from the house of William C. Love to the Huntingdon road on the Carroll County line, and also one from the same place to Nash's Bluff, on the Middle Fork of Forked Deer River.

At the April (1825) term roads were ordered opened from Gibsonport to Jackson, Dresden, Lexington, and Obion County. These were the first roads opened in the county.

The number of acres of land reported for taxation in 1824 was 273,163. A great deal of this land was owned by nonresidents. The rate of taxation on each 100 acres of land was 12 1-2 cents; on each town lot, 25 cents; on each slave between twelve and fifty years old, 16 2-3 cents; on each four-wheeled carriage, $3.33 1-3; on each two-wheeled carriage, $1.66 2-3. The tax lists showed only forty-six slaves and sixty-nine white polls. The revenue derived from all sources was $885.85. (Minutes of County Court.)

Sixteen years afterwards (in 1840), when the assessment was made upon the value of the land, I find the following figures: Number of acres assessed, 256,086, valued at $894,869, or nearly $3.50 per acre; the aggregate value of personal property was $628,225, and the tax collected was $6,350.09.

Twenty years from this time (in 1860) the number of acres assessed was 400,019, valued at $4,238,519; the value of town lots was $233,765; the value of personal property, including slaves, was $2,993,514; making the total taxables of the county, $7,465,798.

In 1830 the population of the county was 5,801; in 1840 it was 13,689; in 1850 it was 19,548; in 1860 it was 21,777; in 1870 it was 25,666; in 1880 it was 32,685; in 1890 it was 35,859; in 1900 it was 39,408.

The log courthouse, built in 1824, stood five years. In 1829 it was replaced by a two-story brick building, which cost the county about $6,000. This building stood until 1837, when, being deemed unsafe, it was taken down, and a temporary courthouse was erected out of the material.

In 1839 the contract was let for the erection of a new and commodious building suitable to the wants of the county. The contractors upon this building were Robert Shaw and Robert Jetton, the latter an uncle of the present Mr. J. W. Jetton, of Trenton. This courthouse was completed in 1841, at a total cost to the county of $20,000.

Here is a picture of this courthouse, which stood for fifty-eight years as the temple of justice of the county. It was removed in 1899, and the present handsome and convenient structure was erected in its place.

The construction of the lines of the Louisville and Nashville Railroad and the Mobile and Ohio Railroad through the county in 1857-1859 gave an immense impetus to the growth and development of the county. Prior to this time the surplus products of the county were conveyed by wagon to Hickman, Ky., on the Mississippi River, and goods and supplies were obtained from the same point. Eaton, on the Middle Fork of the Forked Deer River, became a considerable shipping place, and quantities of cotton and other products were hauled to this point and transported in keel boats to the Mississippi

OLD COURTHOUSE.

River. When the railroads were built, all this traffic ceased; Hickman and Eaton lost their consequence as ports of entry and egress for Gibson County, and their greatness became a memory. The two railroads mentioned passed through some of the best agricultural lands of the county, and brought these lands into close contact with the great markets of the country, North and South. The Mobile and Ohio Railroad, especially, was located through the most fertile portion of the county. This road, passing through the entire length of the county, from north to south, had a greater influence upon agricultural development than any other road.

The Illinois Central Railroad completed its

line through the county in 1872, thus giving the county three important lines of railway, and affording means of transportation and market facilities unsurpassed by any county in the State.

The present state of progress and development in Gibson County is largely due to its railroads. I know of no county in this State or any other State that serves better to illustrate the influence of railroads upon production and the formation of social and business conditions than Gibson County. The population of the county has doubled since the advent of railroads; a number of towns, some of them important places of trade and manufacture, owe their existence to the railroads; facility of transportation and easy access to the great consuming centers of the country vastly increased the volume and variety of agricultural products, so that every season of the year had its distinctive activities fostered and stimulated by market demands and the wondrous capability of the soil; business opportunities and industrial occupations were multiplied, and every social interest was advanced. No wonder that Gibson County, at the beginning of the last decade, stood as the fifth county in the State in point of population, and first as owing all her consequence to her purely agricultural interests.

RESIDENCE OF G. R. HOWSE, NOTED STOCKMAN, TRENTON.

RESIDENCE OF A. R. DODSON, CASHIER MERCHANTS' STATE BANK, HUMBOLDT.

GIBSON COUNTY TO-DAY.

PEN AND PICTURE SKETCHES.

My aim in presenting the following pen and picture sketches of people and things in the Gibson County of to-day, as I see them, is to bring before the mind's eye the state of social, commercial, and industrial growth the county has reached during the seventy-six years of its existence as a civic organization.

An exhaustive presentation of the processes which have brought about the present advanced state of development along all lines of substantial improvement is not attempted and would be impracticable in a work of this kind. Hence, I shall ask the reader to be satisfied with a glance, as it were, at those things in picture and print, which stand as the indices of progress.

Gibson County contains something near six hundred square miles of territory. It has a population, according to the United States census of 1900, of 39,408, or a little over sixty-five persons to the square mile; thus exceeding the general ratio of population in the State, which is only forty-eight to the square mile of territory.

Gibson County is strictly an agricultural county. It has no minerals, so far as is known, and no definite strata of hard rock, such as limestone, slate, or sandstone. Occasional limited beds of coarse reddish or brown sandstone are met with, but the county, as well as all of West Tennessee, is remarkable for the absence of rock formation. The surface of the county is considerably diversified by hill, plain, and valley, though there are no high hills as in other portions of the State. The hilly portion of the county is confined almost entirely to the eastern half; but even here the hills are not formidable, and there is no part so rugged that it cannot be utilized for some useful agricultural purpose. These broken lands of the county are poor compared with the level and valley lands, but, if properly cared for, will well repay cultivation. There is much good land in the valleys and level spaces that occur on the east side, and some of the best farms and most prosperous farmers are to be found here. The western half of the county is generally level or gently rolling, and is distinctively the best farming portion of the county as a whole.

The line of the Mobile and Ohio Railroad, passing from north to south nearly centrally through the county, marks closely the dividing line between the best lands and those that are not so good by reason of physical formation. All over the county, however, the soil may be said to be productive, even in the poorest sections, though it differs vastly in productiveness. The soil upon the surface is loam, more or less mixed with sand and siliceous matter, and rests upon a subsoil of clay. In many places on the west side the surface soil is almost pure loam. The surface soil over the county varies in depth from six inches to twenty-four inches, and the depth of the clay subsoil is from eighteen inches to four feet. Below the clay in almost all parts of the county is found a stratum of sand, and below the sand very hard and impervious clay is found.

The soil of Gibson County is generally very mellow and easily cultivated, and also easily moved by washing; so that the farmer must exercise care, if he would preserve his farm from becoming a network of gullies.

The county has no specialty in the way of agricultural production. It is adapted to diversified farming, and, on account of climatic conditions, is capable of producing a wider range of farm products than many other portions of our country. Cotton, tobacco, all the cereals and grains, vegetables, and fruits grow and mature here in perfection. For several years past the strawberry and tomato crops of the county have been a source of great revenue to the farmers. The northwest section of the county is famous for its wheat production, while the southern and southwestern sections are equally celebrated for their corn and cotton. Improved herds of cattle and hogs roam the pastures everywhere, while thoroughbred saddle and harness horses are taking the place of the scrub breeds of a bygone age. In a word, Gibson is a first-class agricultural county, and is becoming better every day.

There are but few water courses in the county, yet water for domestic and farm use is obtained easily and cheaply. Pure freestone water for domestic use is secured from wells sunk to a depth of from twenty-five feet to forty feet; the supply is inexhaustible. Water for stock, away from the streams, is obtained from ponds, which are easily constructed. The principal water courses of the county are the Middle Fork and the North Fork of the Forked Deer River and the South Fork and the Rutherford Fork of the Obion River. There are a number of smaller streams, tributary to these, but none of particular note.

The county was once very heavily timbered, but in recent years the great demand for timber and timber products, together with the subjection of the lands to agricultural uses, has very greatly reduced the quantity and quality of the timber resources of the county; still, there is an abundance left for all purposes.

MAGISTRATES OF GIBSON COUNTY.

COUNTY GOVERNMENT.

The county is divided into twenty-five civil divisions, or districts, in each of which two magistrates are elected biennially. Each incorporated city or town also elects one or more magistrates. Trenton and Milan elect two each, and Humboldt, Dyer, and Rutherford elect one each; making the entire magistracy of the county consist of fifty-seven members. The magistrates of the county constitute the

County Court, or legislative assembly of the county, having statutory jurisdiction over county affairs. The chairman of this court, elected by the members, is the judge of the County Court. This court holds four regular terms each year—on the first Mondays of January, April, July, and October.

The members of the County Court, with postoffice address, are given below:

District No. 1: J. H. Barnwell, Medina; R. A. Caldwell, Medina. District No. 2: H. H. Bass, Gibson; H. H. Love, Humboldt. District No. 3: W. N. L. Dunlap, Humboldt; John C. Adams, Humboldt; W. N. Bennett, Fruitland. District No. 4: W. L. Kilzer, Gibson Wells; W. F. Jones, Gibson Wells. District No. 5: J. R. Thompson, Brazil; B. W. Sappington, Brazil. District No. 6: J. W. Smith, Eaton; J. H. Hall, Eaton. District No. 7: R. Z. Taylor, Trenton; W. S. Crafton, Trenton; J. I. Crenshaw, Trenton; W. E. Seat, Trenton: District No. 8: H. L. Wyatt, Yorkville; J. T. Carlton, Neboville. District No. 9: W. J. R. Becton, Rutherford; E. J. Smithson, Rutherford; W. P. Young, Rutherford. District No. 10: J. W. Howell, Kenton; W. A. Montgomery, Kenton. District No. 11: J. W. Phelan, Laneview; J. M. Richmond, Dyer. District No. 12: W. A. McLean (dead, and vacancy not filled); T. W. Branson, Trenton. District No. 13: R. E. Edwards, Milan; A. Jordan, Milan; E. N. Stone, Milan, J. J. Collins, Milan. District No. 14: M. Brown, Bradford; J. S. Alexander, Bradford. District No. 15: J. A. Gilliland, Gann; J. M. Williamson, Hollyleaf. District No. 16: J. W. Coleman, Trenton; C. W. Harrison, Trenton. District No. 17: F. J. Bruff, Bradford; A. H. Holmes, Bradford. District No. 18: J. H. Hunt, Gibson; J. A. Paris, Cedar. District No. 19: D. Witherington, Rutherford; O. McDaniel, Rutherford. District No. 20: Sam. Mitchell, Fruitland; J. H. Koffman, Fruitland. District No. 21: D. J. Hutchinson, Dyer; J. D. Gardner, Dyer; J. A. McLeod, Dyer. District No. 22: J. M. Ford, Idlewild; J. N. Thetford, Idlewild. District No. 23: N. B. Johnston, Edmunds; H. L. Belew, Edmunds. District No. 24: W. B. Tilghman, Tyson; John Q. Temple, Mason Hall. District No. 25: W. W. Wade, Brazil; A. H. Fitzgerald, Trenton.

The present county officers are:

Judge of County Court, J. D. Hutchinson.

Clerk of County Court, R. J. Dow.

Clerk of Circuit Court, J. W. Vick.

Sheriff, R. E. Morgan.

Trustee, W. F. McRee.

Register, G. W. Ingram.

Clerk and Master, Chancery Court, Legrand W. Jones.

Surveyor, W. H. Dodd.

Coroner, W. W. Harrison.

Ranger, W. E. Seat.

County Physician, Dr. T. J. Happel.

Road Commissioner, G. R. Casey.

Superintendent of Schools, J. B. Cummings.

Members of State Legislature: Dr. A. E. Turner, Senator; L. W. Morgan and E. N. Stone, Representatives.

The county's Representative in the Congress of the United States is Hon. Rice A. Pierce, of Obion County. The county is in the Ninth Congressional District, composed of the counties of Gibson, Dyer, Lake, Lauderdale, Obion, Haywood, Crockett, and Weakley.

The county is in the Eighteenth Judicial Circuit, composed of the counties of Carroll, Crockett, Gibson, and Haywood. Judge John R. Bond, of Haywood County, is circuit judge, and Hon. W. W. Wade, of Gibson County, attorney-general.

The Eleventh Chancery Division, in which Gibson is situated, is composed of the counties of Dyer, Fayette, Gibson, Haywood, Lauderdale, Obion, Tipton, and Weakley. John S. Cooper, of Gibson County, is chancellor.

NEW COURTHOUSE.

The new courthouse of the county, just completed, is a building that in beauty of design, architectural finish, and convenience of arrangement will compare with any in the State. It fitly represents the progressive spirit of the people of the county. It is in all respects a modern structure, designed and constructed with an intelligent and comprehensive regard for the wants of a great and growing county.

The following account of the laying of the corner stone of the new courthouse is taken from the columns of the "Herald-Democrat" of Friday, October 20, 1899:

"According to previous announcement, the exercises of laying the corner stone of our new courthouse took place here last Wednesday. After an ugly day of lowering clouds and downpour of rain, Wednesday morning dawned as beautiful as a May day, with cool and crisp temperature. The work was to be done under the auspices of the Masonic fraternity, and some weeks ago Trenton Lodge No. 86 sent out invitations to every lodge and Mason in Gibson County, together with some outside of the county. Early Wednesday morning they began to arrive from all directions, by trains and private conveyances, until the number of Masons alone was estimated to be over three hundred. In addition to these, hundreds of citizens from all parts of Gibson County were here to witness the interesting event and to show their interest in the seat of the county government and our magnificent temple of justice.

"According to programme the Grand Lodge

opened in their hall at 11 o'clock and formed a procession, headed by a brass band, marching south on College street to Fourth street, thence west to High street, thence north to Eaton street, thence east to the Square, and around the Square to the northeast corner of the courthouse, where the corner stone is situated. There the beautiful ceremonies were gone through with by Grand Master Bullock and his officers. Many papers, articles, and interesting documents, read out by Hon. A. W. Biggs, were placed in the corner stone, among which were: Copper plate, which was in the corner stone of the first Masonic Temple in Trenton, containing the names of the officers of Trenton Lodge No. 86, at that time, as follows: A. S. Currey, Worshipful Master; S. W. Sharp, Senior Warden; and Robert P. Caldwell, Junior Warden. This plate contained also the names of the officers of Trenton Chapter No. 36, Royal Arch Masons— Nelson I. Hess, High Priest; C. J. Bradley, King; and J. C. Gillespie, Scribe— and the names of the officers of the Grand Lodge of Tennessee, as follows: R. L. Caruthers, Grand Master; John S. Dashiel, Grand Secretary. On the reverse side of this plate were engraved the names of the present officers of Trenton Lodge No. 86 —Dr. Z. Biggs, Worshipful Master; R. E. Grizzard, Senior Warden; G. B. Hicks, Junior Warden; M. Morris, Secretary—and the names of the following Grand Lodge officers: M. W. Joseph Bullock, Grand Master; R. W. J. R. Smith, Grand Junior Warden; R. W. J. B. Garrett, Grand Secretary. The names of the present county officials, the Building Committee, the architects, the contractors, and the chairman of the County Court are also placed in the corner stone, as were copies of the newspapers of Gibson County, the Daily American, and the Commercial Appeal; a copper plate containing names of the members of the bar of Gibson County; a roster of the County Court; the business enterprises of Trenton; photographs of the old courthouse; together with a bottle of wine, coins, the first postal note issued at Trenton post office, a twenty-five-cent shinplaster, a Confederate bill, several advertising cards, photographs of President and Mrs. McKinley, and a calendar for 1899.

RESIDENCE OF G. W. WADE, OF THE LAW FIRM OF WADE & WADE, TRENTON.

"After these ceremonies were finished, Hon. W. I. McFarland was introduced and delivered an able address, which was greatly enjoyed and appreciated by the large audience. At the conclusion of Mr. McFarland's address, A. W. Biggs, in behalf of the ladies of Trenton, presented him with a beautiful bouquet. Mr. McFarland responded feelingly and eloquently to the compliment.

"The lines were then reformed and the procession marched to Hotel Bigelow, where a fine dinner was waiting. Some four hundred guests were fed there, after which the procession dispersed. A good band discoursed music for the occasion.

"The dismissal of Peabody High School and the attendance of teachers and pupils in a body was no small feature of the occasion.

"Altogether it was a gala day for Trenton, and one long to be remembered."

The erection of this splendid edifice was attained after considerable effort on the part of the progressive citizens of the county, and not without a good deal of opposition from the ultra-conservative element of the county. But after the building had been completed it became the pride of all the people. The building was completed and the keys delivered to the county authorities on Monday, July 1, 1901. The ceremonies attending the delivery of the keys and the dedication of the building were of an interesting character and were witnessed by a large concourse of citizens assembled in the large Circuit Court room of the building.

COL. R. Z. TAYLOR.

If credit is due to any one man more than to others for the new and beautiful, as well as commodious and modern, courthouse building, which is now the pride of Gibson County, it is to Col. R. Z. Taylor, of Trenton. For many years the old courthouse has been inadequate for the business of this large and constantly growing county, and had become dangerous to be used. The County Court had voted down a proposition to erect a new courthouse building, and it was apparent to all that remodeling the old one would not suffice. There was needed some one to take hold of the matter, work up the sentiment for a new building, then get the County Court to act upon it, and build.

When the Methodist Conference was held at Trenton in 1897, a large crowd of preachers and laymen from all over West Tennessee attended, and among the number of laymen was Col. A. W. Stovall, of Jackson, who, being struck with the beauty of Trenton, its churches and residences, as well as by the dilapidated courthouse building, on his return to his home wrote a poem on the "Old Courthouse at Trenton," which was published in one of the Jackson papers and copied in the county papers all over West Tennessee. This poem was too much for Colonel Taylor, and he at once announced himself as a candidate for membership in the County Court, and was elected. No sooner had he been elected than he began to agitate the building of a new courthouse, and at the January (1899) term a committee was appointed to enter into a contract for the building of the new courthouse; and Judge F. D. Bryant, then the chairman, appointed Messrs. R. Z. Taylor, T. J. Happel, J. T. Hale, of Trenton; B. C. Jarrell, of Humboldt; and J. W. Howell, of Kenton, as the committee. This committee has been retained, with one change, caused by the death of Mr. B. C. Jarrell; and, in his stead, his son, Mr. J. R. Jarrell, a well-known and prominent business man of Humboldt, was appointed.

The courthouse is now completed, and it is said to be the finest courthouse building in the State.

Colonel Taylor was born in Medon, Madison County, Tenn., on February 24, 1846; was the oldest son of the late B. M. Taylor. His father moved to Gibson County, Tenn., in October, 1848, and he was therefore reared and educated in this county. In January, 1864, he enlisted in the Confederate Army, and surrendered at Gainsville, Ala., on May 15, 1865. On his return from the war he settled at Trenton, and in 1869 he married Miss Mettie Ivie, the daughter of Mr. E. G. Ivie. The success of Colonel Taylor is due in no small measure to Mrs. Taylor, who is a woman of great force of character, as well as one of many charming graces.

In 1869 he was admitted to the bar, and moved to Mt. Vernon, Ill., where his father had large land interests, at which place he remained for several years, practicing his profession and selling off the lands belonging to his father, Judge Williams' estate, and others.

Returning to Trenton in 1872 he resumed the practice of law, and remained in the active practice until appointed by Chancellor Livingston as Clerk and Master of the Chancery Court at Trenton, in August, 1887. He served two terms as Clerk and Master, and upon the expiration of his second term he resumed the practice of law at Trenton, forming a partnership with Mr. Albert W. Biggs, under the firm name of Taylor & Biggs.

For about fourteen years Colonel Taylor was the chairman of the Democratic Executive Committee of Gibson County, and has always taken an active interest in politics. He is prominently identified with many business enterprises at Trenton; is a member of the firm of Taylor, Enochs & Co., and was a member of the firm of D. C. Taylor & Co., and has large farming interests.

Colonel Taylor is a man of many lovable traits of character, and is universally esteemed and admired by a large circle of friends and acquaintances. He has a large family, and lives in a beautiful home in the suburbs of Trenton.

RESIDENCE OF W. N. L. DUNLAP, ESQ., CLERK AND MASTER, HUMBOLDT LAW COURT, HUMBOLDT.

GIBSON COUNTY AND THE JUDICIARY.

From its organization Gibson County has been noted for the high standing of its bar. Before and since the war the bar of the county has been prominently connected with the judiciary of the State. Ever since the Constitution of 1870 was adopted this county has had a representative upon the Supreme Bench; and likewise since that time it has had representatives almost continuously on the bench of the inferior courts, and part of the time three judges from this bar have been in active service at the same time. The bar has been noted not only for its learning and ability, but for its integrity, professional courtesy, and admirable citizenship.

Judge A. O. P. Totten was one of the early members of the bar at Trenton, and was a noted lawyer in his day. Prior to the war he was made a member of the Supreme Court and served with distinction. At the time of his elevation to the Supreme Bench he was a resident of Madison County, but had resided there only a short time, and Gibson County has always claimed him because she made him. It is regretted that a cut cannot be obtained for this work.

Judge Samuel Williams was a pioneer in the practice of law at Trenton. He had a wide reputation and practiced in many of the courts in the other counties of the State.
He was noted for his accuracy in the knowledge of the law and his pointed application of legal principles. In 1858 he was elected circuit judge, and held the office until the courts were closed by the Civil War. While in this office he evinced those peculiar characteristics that go to make up a good judge.

Maj. R. P. Caldwell became a member of the Trenton bar before the war. He was one of the big-brained lawyers of the State, and was especially noted for his powerful ability to present issues of fact before a jury. He was a diamond in the rough. In 1858 he was elected attorney-general and held the position until the breaking out of the Civil War. As a prosecuting attorney the State has had few men that were his equal. He entered the Confederate service and rose to the rank of major.

JUDGE SAMUEL WILLIAMS.

After the war he turned his attention somewhat to politics and was a member of Congress from the district of which Gibson County was a part.

Judge John L. Williamson was for a long time a member of the bar at Trenton. He was noted for his brilliancy and wit as well as his high legal attainments. In 1867 he was appointed chancellor, which place, however, he held for only a short time. He resigned the office to resume his practice, which was large and lucrative.

Judge Gideon B. Black came to Gibson County in the early fifties and began the practice of law at Trenton. He was a noted lawyer before the war, and was perhaps the best reader of human nature that ever practiced law in the county. He might well be termed "the rough and ready" of the Gibson County bar. At the breaking out of the war he entered the Confederate service, and at the close was a colonel of one of the noted Tennessee regiments. At the first election after the adoption of a new Constitution in 1870, he was elected circuit judge, and served for a term of eight years. He was a just and upright judge.

JUDGE JOHN L. WILLIAMSON.

Judge Thomas J. Freeman was a native-born Gibson Countian, and began the practice of law at Trenton before the war. He was a brilliant and earnest debater, and took an active part in politics. He was a soldier in the Confederate army, and by the close of the war had risen to the rank of colonel. In 1870 he was elected to the Supreme Bench for a term of eight years. In 1878 he was re-elected, and was a member of that court when the memorable "103" case—the bondholders against the taxpayers—was decided, and his opinion in that case is an evidence of his legal ability and his accurate knowledge of the great legal principles that underlie republican government.

Judge John T. Carthel began the practice of his profession at Trenton before the war, and at the breaking out of the war he and his brother were doing a splendid practice. Judge Carthel was noted not only for his legal ability, but for the forcefulness of his character and his polite and courtly bearing. He entered the Civil War and was a captain in the Confederate army. After the war he resumed practice at Trenton, and was one of the most successful members of the bar. In 1874 he was made a member of the Supreme Court Commission, a court established to assist the Supreme Court in disposing of its overburdened docket. On this commission he served with credit and distinction. In 1878 he was elected circuit judge, and occupied the bench for eight years. He was a vigorous, courtly, just, and upright judge.

JUDGE THOMAS J. FREEMAN.

Judge W. C. Caldwell began the practice of law at Trenton in 1878, and practiced with success until 1883, when he was made a member of the Court of Referees, another court created to relieve the Supreme Court docket. He served with much distinction in this position and made such a favorable impression that at the general election in 1886 he was elected a judge of the Supreme Court for the State at large, and in 1894 was re-elected for a second term, and he is at present a member of the Supreme Court. His opinions evidence the high type of his legal ability, and, on commercial law especially, are regarded as very high authority. He has served on the bench eighteen years, and is still quite a young man.

JUDGE JOHN T. CARTHEL.

JUDGE W. C. CALDWELL.
(Of Supreme Court of State of Tennessee).

Judge John S. Cooper began the practice of law at Trenton in 1870, and from the beginning took high rank as a lawyer. He was quite successful as a general practitioner, but he was specially noted for his preference for chancery practice, in which line he was eminently successful. He was more than once appointed special judge of the Supreme Court and the inferior courts. He was mayor of the city of Trenton, and for one term a State senator.

JUDGE JOHN S. COOPER
(Chancellor of Chancery Division).

In 1894 he was elected chancellor, which position he now holds. He has made an enviable reputation as chancellor, and won the esteem of the bar and the people. In the midst of the busy rounds of the active practice of his profession, he has found the time to devote himself to literary pursuits. He is not only well read and scholarly, but has also contributed articles of literary worth and merit to the press.

Judge M. M. Neil began the practice of law at Trenton in partnership with Judge John T. Carthel, and when Judge Carthel was made a member of the Com-

JUDGE M. M. NEIL.
(Of Chancery Court of Appeals).

mission Court the whole burden of their practice fell upon him, and though quite a young man he was equal to the occasion. He was one of the most successful, courteous, and painstaking lawyers that ever practiced at the Trenton bar. He had a State reputation as a splendid lawyer. In 1895, when the Court of Chancery Appeals was created, he was appointed by Governor Turney as one of the members of that court. In 1896 he was nominated for the place without opposition, and in the general election was elected, and is at present a member of that court. He has the reputation of being one of the most thorough, industrious, and learned judges that has occupied a place on the courts of appellate jurisdiction.

Gen. W. W. Wade is a native of Gibson County. His ancestors settled in the county at an early day, and were among those early settlers who opened and developed this great section of the State. In early life he suffered a severe affliction in the loss of one of his legs, but this in no way daunted his energy or his ambition. In 1881 he began the practice of law at Trenton, and at once gave evidence of those characteristics which go to make up a really successful lawyer. He was mayor of the city for one term. He was recorder of the city, and was twice elected as a member of the General Assembly of the State. In 1891 he was appointed attorney-general of the new judicial circuit created that year, and in 1892 was elected by the people for the balance of the judicial term. In 1894, at the general election, he was re-elected for the term of eight years. He enjoys the reputation of being one of the most vigorous, active, and well-balanced attorneys-general in the State.

The connection that Gibson County has had with the judiciary of the State, as evidenced by the long list above enumerated, speaks volumes for the character and reputation of the legal profession in Gibson County and shows the character of the citizenship of the county.

PORTRAITS AND BRIEF SKETCHES OF PRESENT COUNTY OFFICERS.

Dr. A. E. Turner.

Dr. A. E. Turner, of Neboville, Gibson County, Tenn., was born in Alamance County, N. C., in 1853, and was educated at Wilson Academy, Melville, N. C. He read medicine under Dr. B. F. Mebane, of Mebaneville, N. C., and graduated from the Medical Department of the University of Pennsylvania on March 13, 1874. He emigrated soon afterwards to Tennessee and located at what is now known as "Neboville," a small

DR. A. E. TURNER
(Member of State Senate from Gibson County).

town in Gibson County, which has been built up in the last few years. Soon after his location in Tennessee he married Miss M. M. Banks, of Gibson County, and resulting from this marriage he has two daughters and two sons. One daughter, Blanche, is now married to Dr. F. E. Wyatt, of Yorkville, Tenn.; one son is now at the University of Tennessee; and one son and one daughter are at home.

Dr. Turner has all these years continuously engaged in the practice of his profession. He has also engaged in farming, and is known in his county as one of the largest and most successful farmers in the county, paying especial attention to raising Jersey and short-horned cattle. He has at all times taken an active part in politics, and in every election since he came to Tennessee he has contributed his part to the success of the Democratic party. In 1898 he was elected on the Democratic ticket State Senator from Gibson and Crockett Counties, and again indorsed in 1900, being now a member of the State Senate. It was through Dr. Turner's personal effort that the four-mile law was extended to towns of two thousand inhabitants and under, in 1899.

Dr. Turner's ancestors were Scotch-Irish and emigrated to this country in 1755, and settled in Virginia. When he returns home after the close of this session of the Legislature, he will resume his professional duties. He is a director in the Farmers and Merchants' Bank at Newbern, Tenn.

Dr. Turner has taken a lively interest in educational matters always, and has been largely instrumental in building up Nebo High School, at Neboville, Tenn., having been secretary of the school board ever since its establishment in 1890; in fact, he takes a part in every public enterprise. He has been a successful financier and has accumulated enough of this world's goods to keep the wolf from the door.

He is a member of the Knights of Pythias, Knights Templar, and I. O. O. F., and a member of the Cumberland Presbyterian Church.

Hon. L. W. Morgan.

L. W. Morgan, member of the State Legislature from Gibson County, was born in Henry County, Tenn., on August 5, 1854. When about seven years old he moved with his parents to Gibson County, and was brought up on a farm, receiving such literary education as the common schools of the county afforded. Although denied the benefit of a collegiate education, yet such was the strength of his natural ability that by application he became a thorough English scholar, supplementing this by the development of rare business qualities. From early life he has devoted himself to the business of farming, in which he has been quite successful. Beginning in life with no capital, save his own indomitable purposes and excellent judgment, he has become one of the largest landowners and most extensive farmers and stock breeders in the county.

In 1897 Mr. Morgan was elected, by the County Court of Gibson County, to the office of county surveyor, serving acceptably in that

HON. L. W. MORGAN
(Member of Legislature from Gibson County).

position for a period of three years, when his fellow-citizens chose him to represent them in the State Legislature, being elected to that position in the fall of 1900, and is at present a member of that body.

In 1886 Mr. Morgan married Miss Lula Gause, a most estimable lady and a member of a most prominent family of Brownsville, Haywood County, Tenn. They have five children living, all of whom give promise of becoming bright and useful members of society.

Mr. Morgan is a member of the Christian Church, also of the Masonic fraternity, and in politics he is a Democrat. In the business and social world Mr. Morgan is known and esteemed for his punctuality and honesty, his word being as good as his bond; in public affairs he is always in the forefront of progress; and in matters of social obligations no duty is left unfulfilled. With the people of Gibson County Mr. Morgan is quite popular.

D. J. Hutchinson.

D. J. Hutchinson was born five miles northwest of Trenton, Gibson County, Tenn., on January 8, 1853. His early life was spent on the farm with his father, near what is now known as Grizzard. His opportunities for an education were limited; but, by the use of diligence and walking three or four miles to school, he managed to secure a fair common-school education.

In 1874 he moved with his father to Southwest Missouri, where he spent one year; during his stay there he taught one term in a public school. He returned to Gibson County in 1875, where for a long time he worked on a farm, and was timber contractor for the Mobile and Ohio Railroad between Trenton and Dyer.

On September 13, 1877, he was married to Miss Nannie A. Grier, of Dyer, Tenn., and soon after he bought a farm one mile northwest of Dyer and moved there, where he still resides.

In 1883 he joined the Cumberland Presbyterian Church, at Mt. Olive, and was soon made a ruling elder in that congregation; he has also served several years as superintendent of his Sunday school.

D. J. HUTCHINSON
(Judge of County Court).

In 1895 he was elected justice of the peace, which office he filled with such satisfaction that he was reëlected in 1900.

He and his wife lived happily together for some twenty-three years, and their home was blessed with fourteen children; but on December 19, 1900, his wife was called away by death, which was a great loss to him and which cast over his home quite a gloom.

He had the honor of being elected chairman of the County Court of Gibson County at its January (1901) term, and he seems to take great delight in transacting the business of the office.

Judge Hutchinson enjoys sober habits, using no strong drinks; and he and his entire family are free from the use of tobacco.

In politics he is a Democrat, and is a strong advocate of the principles as taught by W. J. Bryan. His opposition to Cleveland caused him to vote with the Populist party during one campaign.

During the life of the Agricultural Wheel and Farmers and Laborers' Union, Esquire Hutchinson was a very prominent member of these organizations, and was for several years their county president, which gave him an opportunity to become acquainted with many farmers in the county. In addition to his farming, he has spent much of his time for the last ten years in buying and shipping cattle and hogs.

Judge Hutchinson is regarded as one of Gibson County's foremost citizens.

R. J. Dew.

R. J. Dew was born on a farm near Lebanon, Wilson County, Tenn., on September 18, 1842. When a lad his parents, Davis Swift and Ruth Don Carlos Dew, moved to Weakley County, where his boyhood days were spent on a farm near Dresden. He received in the schools of that day a limited education.

At the age of eighteen years Mr. Dew joined the Confederate Army as a private in the first company of Weakley County Volunteers—the "Old Hickory Blues;" was in the organization of the Ninth Tennessee Volunteer Infantry at Jackson in May, 1861; took part with his regiment—which composed part of Maj. Gen. B. F. Cheatham's Division—in all the battles fought, except that of Perryville, Ky., on October 8, 1862; was twice wounded—first, at Chickamauga, Ga., on September 19, 1863, and again at Missionary Ridge, Tenn., on November 25, 1863; and, as captain of the company then composed of the remnant of the old Ninth Regiment, surrendered, at the close of the war, with the army commanded by Gen. Joseph E. Johnston, at Greensboro, N. C., on April 26, 1865.

R. J. DEW
(Clerk of County Court).

After the close of the war he returned to Tennessee and located on a farm near Eaton, Gibson County.

While he was a soldier he professed conversion and, in August, 1866, joined the Baptist Church at Spring Hill, Gibson County.

He was married to Miss Amanda Ferriss on January 8, 1868, from which union five children were born, three of whom are living—Anna H., Carlos F., and Minnie Maud.

He moved with his family to Trenton in 1887, for the purpose of educating his children; engaging in various pursuits until August, 1898, at which time he was elected clerk of the County Court of Gibson County, which position he now holds.

W. F. McRee.

W. F. McRee, eldest son of John I. and Cynthia McRee, was born in Carroll County, Tenn., near Christmasville, on January 4, 1842. He moved to Gibson County, three and one-half miles south of Trenton, in February, 1846, where he has since resided. He received his education at the "Old Field School."

Mr. McRee enlisted in Company G, Forty-seventh Tennessee Regiment, in November, 1861, and was paroled at Augusta, Ga., in May, 1865. While under Joseph E. Johnston, at Hope Hill Church on May 28, 1864, he was severely wounded.

After he returned from the war, he clerked at Trenton, Tenn., until January, 1872, when

W. F. M'REE
(Trustee).

he returned to the farm and married Miss Lockie M. Johnston, who died in October, 1879. By this union he had one son and two daughters.

In September, 1881, he married Miss Allethia C. Campbell, and by this union he also had one son and two daughters.

He was elected constable of the Seventh District in 1874 and served four years; and in 1879 he was elected justice of the peace and served until 1898, during part of which time (1885-1889) he was chairman of the County Court.

In 1898 he was elected trustee of Gibson County, and was reëlected to the same office in 1900.

Mr. McRee is a Democrat and a member of the old-school Presbyterian Church.

LeGrand W. Jones.

LeGrand W. Jones was born at Huntingdon, Tenn. His parents moved to Trenton when he was a small boy. He was educated at Andrew College and the University of Tennessee. His father, Maj. L. M. Jones, was prominent as a lawyer before the Civil War, and afterwards until declining health compelled him to retire from active practice.

Mr. Jones has been an influential member of the bar of Trenton for a number of years. He ranks among the best lawyers of the State, and enjoys the reputation of being one of the safest counselors and most accurate chancery lawyers at the bar. Since he attained his majority he has taken an active interest in politics, but has cared nothing for political office or preferment. He is a Democrat of the Jeffersonian school, and has devoted much attention to the science and principles of republican government.

In 1882 he married Miss Annie M. Taylor, formerly of Haywood County, Tenn., a member of a very large family of that name, who live principally in Haywood and Fayette Counties.

LEGRAND W. JONES
(Clerk and Master of Gibson Chancery Court).

Upon the organization of the Law Department of the Southwestern Baptist University, at Jackson, Tenn., in 1899, he was elected dean, which position he resigned a year later, not having the time to devote to the position.

In September, 1899, he was appointed

Clerk and Master of the Chancery Court at Trenton, which position he still holds. He is by natural endowments and application well qualified for a judicial position, and his friends predict that he will occupy a place in the judiciary of Tennessee.

Mr. Jones is active in his church relations, and is a leading lay member of the Baptist denomination in this section.

G. W. Ingram.

G. W. Ingram, present Register of Gibson County, is a native of the county, having been born on a farm in the Fifteenth District on August 7, 1860.

He pursued the business of a farmer until August 4, 1894, when he was elected to the office of register; he was reëlected August 4, 1898, and is the present incumbent of the office.

His father, T. J. Ingram, was a Confederate soldier, and lost his life in the service.

Mr. Ingram, who has been selected by his

G. W. INGRAM
(Register of County).

fellow citizens of the county to fill one of the most important offices in their gift, is a man of exemplary character and exceedingly affable and obliging disposition. He is a popular officer.

R. E. Morgan.

R. E. Morgan was born on a farm in Gibson County, Tenn., on September 17, 1866, and remained on the farm till he reached manhood. He comes from good old North Carolina stock, his family being a prominent one in the history of the county. His brother,

R. E. MORGAN
(Sheriff of Gibson County).

Hon. L. W. Morgan, is one of Gibson County's representatives in the Legislature.

In 1890 Mr. Morgan was elected to the position of night police of the city of Trenton, and in 1891 was appointed deputy sheriff and jailer under Sheriff T. L. Hess and served six years in this office. In 1897 he was elected constable in the Trenton district, which office he filled for three years. In August, 1900, he was elected sheriff of the county, succeeding B. F. Jones, which office he still holds.

Mr. Morgan was married to Miss Minnie Thomas, of Trenton, on February 12, 1889. Two children have blessed their union, a boy of ten years and a girl of six years.

Mr. Morgan is a member of the Christian Church in Trenton, and of the Masonic fraternity, and stands high in the county. He is a man of considerable ability, as evidenced by the many positions he has filled.

THE RELIGIOUS INTERESTS OF THE COUNTY.

There is no better criterion of the character of a people than the interest they take in the cause of Christianity. There are at least a hundred houses of worship in Gibson County for white people—one to every six square miles of territory and one to every three hundred and fifty of its white population. The church property of the county will reach a value of $150,000. There are no very costly church buildings in the county, but there are a few very handsome ones, and all are neat and comfortable. It is a pleasure to go over the county and see the clean, white church buildings gleaming among the groves. My space will not admit of an extended chapter on the religious institutions of the county, and I can therefore but glance at this phase of the county's social progress.

Baptist Church.

Although the adherents of the Baptist faith have constituted a large portion of the population of the county since its creation, the church had no distinct local identity until about 1836. Prior to that time the Baptist interests were included in the Western District Association, organized in 1825.

The oldest church organization in the county is Eldad, organized in 1828. The next is Spring Hill, organized in 1832; followed by Old Bethlehem and Poplar Grove, in 1836 and 1838, respectively.

The Central Association was organized at Eldad Church in 1836, with five churches and 163 members.

Now there are 26 churches and 3,560 members, and 1,550 children in the Sunday School. The following exhibit shows the churches, year of organization, membership, and pastor in charge at the present time:

Beech Grove, organized in 1866; members, 123; pastor, J. T. Early.

Bradford, organized in 1875; members, 162; pastor, W. A. Jordan.

Bethel, organized in 1875; members, 70; pastor, J. L. Daws.

Bethpage, organized in 1875; members, 88; pastor, L. McKnight.

Bethlehem, New, organized in 1851; members, 59; pastor, W. A. Jordan.

Bethlehem, Old, organized in 1836; members, 156; pastor (not given).

China Grove, organized in 1852; members, 93; pastor, Edward Watson.

Center, organized in 1874; members, 215; pastor, A. P. Moore.

Chapel Hill, organized in 1846; members, 114; pastor (not given).

Clear Creek, organized in 1850; members, 85; pastor, J. T. Early.

Dyer, organized in 1885; members, 122; pastor, W. A. Jordan.

Eldad, organized in 1828; members, 170; pastor, J. W. Mount.

Gibson, organized in 1877; members, 156; pastor, J. N. Hall.

Hickory Grove, organized in 1863; members, 140; pastor, A. P. Moore.

Humboldt, organized in 1867; members, 205; pastor, L. T. Wilson.

Medina, organized in 1883; members, 103; pastor, W. L. Savage.

Milan, organized in 1867; members, 214; pastor, W. H. Sledge.

Mount Pisgah, organized in 1854; members, 120; pastor, J. W. Crawford.

Mount Pleasant, organized in 1848; members, 141; pastor, A. Nunnery.

Oak Grove, organized in 1870; members, 151; pastor, J. H. Coin.

Oak Wood, organized in 1900; members, 42; pastor, W. H. Sledge.

Poplar Grove, organized in 1838; members, 104; pastor, A. P. Moore.

Salem, organized in 1847; members, 150; pastor, W. A. Jordan.

Spring Hill, organized in 1832; members, 164; pastor, C. D. Jackson.

Trenton, organized in 1850; members, 216; pastor, J. H. Butler.

Unity Grove, organized in 1898; members, 17; pastor, J. T. Early.

Methodist Episcopal Church, South.

Methodism in Gibson County is as old as the county itself. As soon as anything like a social state was formed in the new county, the people began church organizations.

In 1825 or 1826 the Methodists organized a congregation at the house of James Latta, near the present Olive Branch Church.

In 1827 a camp meeting was held at Richardson's Camp Ground, seven miles east of Trenton. In the same year a society was organized at Trenton and trustees were appointed to build a church. This church was completed in 1834 by Thomas Fite.

In 1834 there were five churches comprised in Trenton Circuit, as follows: Trenton, El Bethel, Olive Branch, Clements, and Richardson's Camp Ground.

El Bethel Church was organized in 1827 at the house of William Goodman, four miles north of Milan. This church is now Walnut Grove.

Some of the oldest Methodist churches in the county were: Stanley's Camp Ground, Oak Grove, Zion, Wright's Chapel, Hope Hill, and Antioch; these, with several others, were organized prior to 1850.

The denomination has in Gibson County to-day about thirty churches, with a membership of over thirty-eight hundred, served by eleven pastors. The property of the church in the county is valued at $65,350.

The circuits are divided as follows:

Trenton Circuit — Churches, 5; members, 606; pastor, W. J. Naylor.

Dyer Circuit—Churches, 4; members, 406; pastor, T. J. Simmons.

Milan Circuit—Churches, 4; members, 263; pastor, N. J. Peebles.

Bradford Circuit—Churches, 5; members, 380; pastor, T. W. Hardin.

Medina Circuit—Churches, 5; members, 562.

Trenton Station—Members, 308; pastor, S. L. Jewell.

Dyer Station—Members, 214; pastor, W. W. Armstrong.

Humboldt Station—Members, 360; pastor, R. W. Hood. Humboldt Mission has 196 members.

Milan Station—Members, 248; pastor, J. B. Hardin.

Rutherford Station—Churches, 3; members, 278; pastor, W. Mooney. (This includes Kenton Church.)

The following is a list of the churches in the county:

Trenton Circuit—Olive Branch, Brazil,

FAIRVIEW, RESIDENCE OF JOHN E. CAMPBELL, HUMBOLDT.

Bower's Chapel, Oak Grove, and Pleasant Grove.

Dyer Circuit—Hopewell, Good Hope, Poplar Grove, Greir's Chapel.

Humboldt Mission—Pleasant Hill and Warren's Grove.

Milan Circuit—Salem, Walnut Grove, Moore's Chapel, and ——— Chapel.

Bradford Circuit — Bradford, Chestnut Hill, Antioch, Union.

Medina Circuit—Medina, Zion, Wright's Chapel, and Hope Hill.

Gadsden Circuit—Gibson Station.

Cumberland Presbyterian Church.

Among the first settlers of Gibson County were many Cumberland Presbyterians. These were gradually organized into congregations by itinerant ministers of the church. Rev. N. I. Hess was one of these, preaching in Gibson and adjoining counties. Forked Deer Circuit was one of the first circuits formed in West Tennessee; this was before Gibson County was created. Probably the first church organization in Gibson County was at Yorkville. Rev. S. Y. Thomas was one of the pioneer ministers in the Yorkville neighborhood. The first presbytery covering the church organizations in Gibson County was the Hopewell Presbytery; its first meeting was held at McLemoresville, in Carroll County. The church at Yorkville dates back to 1826 or 1827.

Some of the early ministers of this denomination were Robert Baker, C. Kribbs, R. Burrows, S. Y. Thomas, J. M. Greer, Abner Cooper, and M. Liles.

The denomination has now 23 churches in the county, with a total membership of about 2,500, and 1,400 children in Sunday school.

The following is a list of the churches, with the name of the pastor and number of communicants of each:

Antioch—Members, 74; pastor, W. H. Johns.

Bradford—Members, 18; pastor, W. H. Johns.

Chapel Hill—Members, 29; pastor, O. L. Stockton.

Davidson's Chapel—Members, 80; pastor, W. H. Johns.

Double Springs—Members, 94; pastor, R. W. Oakes.

Dyer—Members, 222; pastor, J. B. Waggoner.

Friendship—Members, 58; pastor, G. W. Anderson.

Humboldt—Members, 157; pastor, Jo McLesky.

Kenton—Members, 150; pastor, J. L. Dickens.

Mayfield—Members, 20; pastor, J. H. Davis.

Medina—Members, 85; pastor, R. W. Oakes.

Milan—Members, 65; pastor, S. A. Sadler.

Morella—Members, 84; pastor, J. L. Dickens.

Mount Olive—Members, 160; pastor, A. S. Johnson.

Pleasant Hill—Members, 70; pastor, Jo McLesky.

Rutherford—Members, 67; pastor, A. S. Johnson.

Trenton—Members, 69; pastor, J. R. George.

Yorkville—Members, 169; pastor, J. L. Cooper.

Beech Grove—Members, 100; pastor, R. W. Oakes.

Cool Springs—Members, 43; pastor, S. B. Zaricor.

Bell's Chapel—Members, 150; pastor, J. A. McIlwain.

North Union—Members, 147; pastor, J. L. Dickens.

Pleasant Green—Members, 123; pastor, J. A. Keaton.

Total number of communicants, 2,334.

Christian Church.

The first Christian churches were organized in the county about 1845. In that year Elder Talbott Fanning, of Nashville, established churches at Trenton, Liberty Grove, and Concord. The denomination now has congregations at Humboldt, Trenton, Milan, Dyer, Rutherford, and at several other points in the county.

The denomination is growing in numbers and influence in the county, and its present membership will reach in the neighborhood of 1,000.

I have not been able to obtain a list of the churches and pastors of this denomination, as it has no general assembly or general organization.

PUBLIC SCHOOLS OF GIBSON COUNTY.

The public school system of Gibson County began to assume definite shape about 1873, upon the passage of the present school law. This law created a State superintendent, a county superintendent in each county, and a uniform system of public schools in the State. It prescribed the method of raising school funds and of building schoolhouses, and provided that the children—white and black—should share equally in the tuition funds of the State and should be taught in separate schools. Under this law the public schools of Gibson County were organized.

John C. Wright, 1887-1889.
A. Killough, 1889-1891.
J. M. Baker, 1891-1895.
Miss Flora Fitzgerald, 1895-1899. (Died on November 14, 1899.)
J. B. Cummins was elected in 1900 and is the present superintendent.

The labor of starting the system and thoroughly organizing the educational work of the county was an arduous task, and it was several years before the system was in thorough working order.

In 1880 the scholastic population of the

THE TEACHERS OF GIBSON COUNTY.
(View taken at session of Teacher's Institute held at Trenton, July 4, 1901.)

The first county superintendent was Dr. W. H. Stilwell, who served under the law passed in 1867. A. S. Curry followed in 1870 and was reëlected in 1873.

The following are the names of those who have served under the present school law:
A. S. Curry, 1873-1875.
Alfred Oliver, 1875-1877.
A. S. Curry, 1877-1879.
J. M. Coulter, 1879-1880. (Resigned.)
James R. Deason, 1880-1885.
A. Kellough, 1885-1887.

county was 11,982, divided as follows: White, 8,705; colored, 3,277. Free schools were pretty generally established over the county, with a few graded schools in the principal towns, as Trenton, Humboldt, and Milan.

As yet the county was poorly supplied with schoolhouses. During Mr. Deason's administration of the office of superintendent, which began in 1880, he was very active in exhorting the people to build schoolhouses, with the result that during his incumbency of the office good school buildings were erected in almost every school district of the county. From that time forward the public school system of the county gained in popularity, and as organization became more perfect, its benefits became more apparent.

In 1891 the Legislature passed an Act requiring all schools to be graded, prescribing the branches to be taught therein. Under this law all the schools of the county were graded.

For the last ten years the public schools of the county have steadily gained in efficiency, due, not only to the perfecting of the general system, but also to the more thorough preparation of teachers for their work. This has been brought about by the establishment of county and district institutes, held under the supervision of the county superintendent, in which the teachers are trained in methods of teaching and the management of schools.

The condition of the public schools of Gibson County is at present very satisfactory. There is probably no county in the State better organized as regards its schools, nor whose school interests are better or more ably managed than those of Gibson County.

Prof. J. B. Cummins, the present superintendent, is a most zealous and efficient worker in the cause of schools. He has eminent

J. B. CUMMINS
(Public School Superintendent).

qualifications for the position of superintendent, acquired by long identification with the schools of the country, to which may be added a natural adaptation to the work. He has been connected with the schools of the county for twenty-seven years as teacher and as assistant in the office of superintendent and in institute work. The school interests of the county under Professor Cummins' management are in a most satisfactory and flourishing condition.

The following figures, taken from the Annual Report of the County Superintendent, show the present state of the schools in Gibson County:

Scholastic population, embracing children, white and colored, from 6 to 21 years of age: White, 11,661; colored, 4,610; total, 16,271.

Enrollment and attendance, 11,746,

RESIDENCE OF HON. JAMES R. DEASON, OF THE FIRM OF DEASON, RANKIN & ELDER, PROMINENT LAWYERS OF TRENTON.

Average daily attendance, 8,078.
Number of schools in county, 157.
Number of teachers employed, 220.
Number of school districts, 77.
Number of schoolhouses, 148.
Average length of schools, 119 days—nearly six months.
Average compensation of teachers per month, $32.21.
Estimated value of all schoolhouses and grounds, $100,180.
Total estimated value of school property, $103,742.
School funds from all sources for 1900, $65,006.
Expenditures, $43,005.
Average cost of tuition per pupil per year, 74 cents.

LANEVIEW ASSEMBLY HALL.

Laneview College.

The establishment of this fine institution for the education of boys and girls is no less a striking proof of the progress made in the matter of education in Gibson County than it is of the enterprise and public spirit of its founders. The school was begun in 1887 upon slender and incomplete resources, but with a determination on the part of its founders to make it an institution in which the youth of the country might obtain the benefits of a collegiate education without undergoing the risk and expense of attending distant colleges. Slowly, but surely, this object has been attained; and now, in the first year of the twentieth century, Laneview College is an accomplished fact and can point with pride to her young men and women graduates, who, by their intellectual and moral attainments, reflect credit upon her as their alma mater.

The cut below represents only the principal assembly room of the College. The institution has its classrooms, chapel, library, and every necessary convenience for successful educational work.

Moore's Hall, an adjunct of the College for young men boarders, is well fitted for their accommodation.

A young ladies' home, for young lady boarders under the care of the matron of the College, is another affix of the institution.

The full course of study embraces the primary, intermediate, and high school grades, together with a full collegiate course, ending with the B.S. degree.

The College is Christian, but nonsectarian, and the moral training of its pupils is held of prime importance.

The situation and environments of the College are such as to invite and stimulate study and develop the intellectual and moral faculties. It is in the midst of rural scenes, where the quiet of nature is undisturbed by the sights and sounds incident to the business and social world; it is surrounded by an enlightened farming community, noted for orderliness and morality. Three handsome churches are almost within sight of the College—Baptist, Methodist, and Presbyterian.

The management of the College, including the Faculty and Board of Managers, is composed of men and women who have the training of children at heart, and who are devoted to the task they have undertaken. They are experienced, capable, and conscientious.

The Faculty is as follows:

J. W. Meadows, Principal.
Rev. W. H. Haste, Jr., Professor of Languages.
Rev. D. B. Jackson, Assistant Principal.
Miss Sallie Blakemore, Primary Department.
Miss Edith G. Ridley, Music.
Mrs. J. W. Meadows, Matron.

Board of Managers:

J. C. Moore, M.D., President.
J. W. Phelan, Esq., Secretary.
F. W. Rawls, Treasurer.

CALENDAR.

First Term begins July 15, 1901.
Second Term begins November 18, 1901.
Commencement Sermon, March 23, 1902.
Celebration of Laneview Literary Society, March 24, 1902.
Eighth Grade Graduating Exercises, March 25, 1902.
Collegiate Graduating Exercises, March 26, 1902.
Concert, March 27, 1902.
Teachers' Training School opens April 1, 1902.

For catalogue and circulars giving full information in regard to course of study, rates, and management of Laneview College, address Prof. J. W. Meadows, Laneview, Gibson County, Tenn.

SOME OF THE MEMBERS OF THE GIBSON COUNTY MEDICAL SOCIETY.

1, Dr. Finis E. Wyatt, Yorkville; 2, Dr. Sydney Thompson, Humboldt; 3, Dr. E. T. Haskins, Tatumville; 4, Dr. J. C. Moore, Laneview; 5, Dr. J. H. Chandler, Humboldt; 6, Dr. J. M. Capps, Lonoke; 7, Dr. T. J. Happel, Trenton; 8, Dr. B. T. Bennett, Trenton; 9, Dr. J. W. Allen, Rutherford; 10, Dr. D. A. Walker, Trenton; 11, Dr. J. B. Rickman, Rutherford; 12, Dr. A. E. Turner, Neboville; 13, Dr. J. T. Faucett, Trenton; 14, Dr. W. J. Barker, Gibson Wells; 15, Dr. J. H. Drane, Dyer.

Gibson County Medical Society.

The Gibson County Medical Society was organized in 1884. At present it has twenty-eight members. John C. Paris is president, and B. T. Bennett is secretary. The society meets quarterly, on the third Tuesdays of March, June, September, and December. It holds three sessions at Trenton and one as decided upon by the secretary.

County Board of Health.

The Board of Health of the county is composed of Dr. T. J. Happel, president; R. J. Dew, County Court Clerk, secretary; and D. J. Hutchinson, chairman of the County Court, who, by virtue of his office, is a member of the Board of Health. Dr. T. J. Happel is the health officer of the county.

It is the province of this board to look after the public health and sanitation, especially epidemic diseases. This duty has been well performed by Dr. Happel, the health officer of the county. Dr. Happel informs me that of the three hundred reported cases of smallpox last year, there has been a mortality of less than one per cent. The entire expense of the health department of the county in the last two years has been only fifteen hundred dollars.

ORGANIZATIONS PROMOTIVE OF THE FARMING INTERESTS OF THE COUNTY.

The Gibson County Fair Association.

The Agricultural and Mechanical Fair Association of Gibson County was organized some twenty-five or thirty years ago, and has been in operation continuously since that time. Its officers and stockholders are, and have always been, among the best men in the county. The association has always offered liberal premiums for almost everything in the agricultural and mechanical line and has always paid its premiums in full.

Its present officers are: Dr. T. J. Happel, president; W. W. Harrison, secretary; W. F. McRee, treasurer.

It holds its fairs annually, usually in the month of October, and lasts about five days.

The Gibson County Farmers' Institute.

The Gibson County Farmers' Institute was organized in August, 1900, and is well supported by the farmers of the county. This organization is destined to accomplish great good to the agricultural interests of the county. It is a most popular institution. The president, William Gay, died in the spring of 1901, after which time the duties of that position devolved on the vice president till its April meeting, when L. D. Spight was elected president. J. H. Koffman is its secretary, and has been since its first organization.

The West Tennessee Horticultural Society.

The West Tennessee Horticultural Society holds its meetings frequently in Gibson County. For many years a citizen of Gibson County was its president. This society has proved of great value in the encouragement and development of the fruit and vegetable interests of the county. It has also done much toward securing better, cheaper, and quicker transportation. Col. J. W. Rosaman, of Gadsden, is its president.

The National Shorthorn Breeders' Association.

The National Shorthorn Breeders' Association is another important adjunct to the farming interests of the county. This is an important society, instituted to promote the breeding of improved breeds of stock, especially shorthorn or Durham cattle. The organization is national in its scope, having members throughout the United States.

The association is in the fourth year of its incorporation under the laws of Tennessee. The registry of shorthorn cattle on the books of the association in the counties of Gibson, Dyer, Obion, Crockett, Chester, and Lauderdale shows more than five hundred head.

The present officers of the association are: Dr. J. A. Griffin, of Crockett County, president; Dr. D. A. Walker, of Trenton, secretary; and W. S. Corbett, assistant secretary.

CITY OF HUMBOLDT.

The city of Humboldt is the largest town in the county of Gibson, and the most important in point of commerce and manufactures. This arises mainly from its superior transportation facilities. It is a railroad town, owing its origin and subsequent growth and development to the two railroads that make this their crossing point.

first merchant and railroad agent of the town. Mr. Gillespie came to the county about 1822, from Maury County, Tenn., and had been engaged in farming prior to coming to Humboldt. He continued to be railroad agent and postmaster at Humboldt until 1869.

Soon after the completion of the Mobile and Ohio Railroad through the county, the

RESIDENCE OF FRANK X. FOLTZ, PROPRIETOR OF HUMBOLDT SPOKE WORKS.

In 1857 the Mobile and Ohio Railroad, which was then building its line through the county, established a depot here, near where Mr. John C. Gillespie, an old citizen of the county, had previously established a small store. Mr. Gillespie was made agent of the road. A small settlement sprang up about the spot, and this seems to have been the beginning of the town of Humboldt. Mr. Gillespie was the pioneer citizen of the place, and was the first postmaster, as well as the

Louisville and Nashville Railroad began building its Louisville and Memphis branch through this portion of the county, and enterprising people saw that the point of crossing of the two roads would, in all probability, become an important place of trade and shipment.

John A. Taliaferro and W. A. Allison erected a steam saw and grist mill on the Mobile and Ohio Railroad near the depot. A land company, composed of J. P. Sharp,

J. N. Lannom, and W. C. Thurston, plotted a large piece of land and sold the lots to persons desiring to establish business enterprises or erect residences. This plot embraced a considerable portion of the present city, including Main street and adjacent streets in the principal business part of the town.

In 1860 the Louisville and Nashville Railroad completed its line, crossing the Mobile and Ohio Railroad several hundred yards north of the spot upon which the Mobile and Ohio depot stood, causing the abandonment of the ground in that locality for building purposes and fixing the site of the future city about the crossing point and upon the higher ground adjacent, north and east. The Osborn plan was perhaps the first land near the crossing laid off in lots. This embraced the portion immediately east of the crossing.

The Sharp, Lannom, and Thurston addition came next. The Roe addition was made on the north, and the T. C. Ferrell addition on the east. A small addition on the south was made by G. W. Wade. The city now covers an area of near two square miles of territory.

In 1861 the little town had made rapid progress and was fast becoming a center of trade and influence, as its promoters had anticipated. But in this year the terrible war between the States began, paralyzing all business enterprise and putting a stop to building and improvement. When peace came, in 1865, the town quickly recovered from the blighting effects of the war; and as social order and settled conditions resumed their sway, business revived, manufactories were established, buildings were erected, and the town grew with astonishing rapidity. In 1870, only five years after the close of the war, the population was over two thousand, and it was the second city in size in the county.

Humboldt to-day has a population of 2,866, being the largest town in the county, and has more manufacturing establishments and a greater number of factory employees than all the other towns of the county combined. There are employed in its various manufactories and shops no less than four hundred people.

The city owns its water works and electric lighting plant, and has a municipal organism highly conducive to the prosperity, progress, and general well-being of the city and its people. The religious institutions of the city are well supported, and the four handsome brick church edifices testify to the zeal and liberality of its Christian people. The city is well laid off and sightly in appearance, and there are many beautiful homes scattered throughout the city and in the suburbs. The city has a system of graded schools inferior to none of its class.

RESIDENCE OF J. J. R. ADAMS, HUMBOLDT.

CITY GOVERNMENT AND CORPORATE HISTORY.

The municipality of Humboldt dates from 1866. In that year the town was incorporated by a sort of "Blanket" Act, which applied also to the towns of Milan and Bristol. The municipal powers conferred upon the town by this Act were enlarged from time to time—first, by decree of the Chancery Court in 1875, and afterwards by Acts of the Legislature—until the town had a fairly efficient system of government.

In 1901 the Legislature gave the city a new general charter, embracing all the essential features of a modern city government and repealing all previous enabling Acts. Under this charter the style of the corporation is "The City of Humboldt," and of its government "The Mayor and Aldermen of the City of Humboldt."

PRESENT CITY GOVERNMENT.

Executive Department.

Neal A. Senter, Mayor.

Legislative Department.

Frank X. Foltz.
John T. Brown.
C. H. Ferrell.
William W. Baird.
Dr. W. H. Mason.

Board of Education.

W. N. L. Dunlap, President.
John E. Campbell.
John S. Lewis.
Hal P. James.
William B. Seat.
Joe H. McDearmon.

Board of Public Works.

(Not yet appointed.)

Board of Health.

Dr. G. W. Penn, President.
Dr. J. H. Preston, Secretary.

Superintendent of Waterworks and Electric Light Plant.

T. G. Scales.

Fire Department.

Outside of a volunteer fire department, which has never been regularly organized, the city has never had a fire department. The city's equipment for the extinguishment of fires consists of the city water mains, with direct pressure from the power house. There are forty water plugs for the attachment of the city hose. The pressure is more than ample to throw two or more streams of water over the highest three-story buildings in the city. The city has 1,200 feet of hose, one hook and ladder truck, one hose wagon, and two hose reels. The city is taking steps to organize active volunteer fire companies at the present time.

Judge of City Court.

Neal A. Senter.

Police Department.

W. E. Blakemore, Chief.
J. J. Atkinson.
George E. Stovall.

HANDSOME MODERN RESIDENCE, PROPERTY OF H. C. READ, OF BIG SPRINGS, TEXAS.

(Mr. Read, being a nonresident, will sell this residence on easy terms—price, $8,500—or will exchange for Texas lands.)

The Mayor is elected for two years, and the members of the City Council, consisting of five members, are elected by the city at large for a term of two years, as well as the City Marshal, Treasurer, Tax Collector, Board of Public Works, and other city officials. The Board of Mayor and Aldermen have the power of appointing the different boards for administering the government of the city. These boards consist of a Board of Public Works, composed of three members; a Board of Education, composed of six members; and a Board of Health, composed of three members.

The Mayor performs the duties of a Recorder; and the Board of Aldermen, under the new charter, elect all policemen, except the Chief of Police, who is elected by the popular vote of the people.

The Mayor is Judge of the City Court, with the jurisdiction of a magistrate in criminal and civil cases. He also has charge of outside city property, except when otherwise provided; and he executes deeds, under seal of the city, to lots in the city cemetery. The Mayor also collects all privilege taxes for the city.

The Board of Public Works has charge of public improvements and of the water works and electric light plant. One of the members of this board is its secretary and one is the chairman of the board. This Board of Public Works has the powers conferred upon it that are usually delegated to a board of its kind.

The new charter, as well as the old one, constitutes the city of Humboldt a special school district, to be managed by a Board of Education, possessed of the powers and authority and performing the same duties as devolve on district directors under the general laws of the State. The members of the Board of Education are elected for a term of three years, and it is so arranged that the term of two members of the board expires each year.

At the organization of the city government under its new charter, in 1901, all the different departments of the city government were put in full and efficient operation, and the system of municipal management thus inaugurated has been eminently conducive to

RESIDENCE OF B. F. JARRELL, HUMBOLDT.

the improvement, growth, and prosperity of the city and to the happiness of its people.

The following is the list of Humboldt's Mayors from 1866 to the present time, with year of installation: Moses E. Senter, 1866; W. E. Allison, 1869; John C. Gillespie, 1873; John M. Camden, 1875; Joseph N. Lannom, 1876; J. C. Hailey, 1878; W. G. Atkins, 1880; W. T. Lenoir, 1881; N. A. Senter, 1882; H. W. Roberts, 1884; L. K. Gillespie, 1886; E. W. Ing, 1890; John T. Crews, 1894; N. A. Senter, unexpired term of John T. Crews, 1897; John A. Collinsworth, 1898; N. A. Senter, present incumbent, 1890.

CHURCHES OF HUMBOLDT.

Baptist Church of Humboldt.

During the year 1867, Rev. D. B. Ray preached occasionally in the old Masonic Hall in Humboldt, and sometime during the summer he was assisted by Rev. J. F. B. Mills in a series of meetings, at the close of which a presbytery was formed and the first Baptist Church was constituted. Rev. D. B. Ray was the first pastor, serving the church about one year, during which time the church was received into the Central Association, at its thirty-first annual session, held with Pleasant Plains Church, Madison County, on September 14. Rev. Moses E. Senter was the second pastor and served the church during a part of 1868 and 1869. He was followed by Rev. I. R. Branham, who became pastor in the summer of 1869 and served until the spring of 1870. He was succeeded by Rev. A. J. Faucett, who remained in the pastorate but a short time, resigning in the summer of 1871. The church again called Rev. Moses E. Senter as pastor, and he served nearly two years, during which time a nice frame building was erected which became the home of the church and was used, though improved from time to time, until 1897. Much credit is due Rev. Moses E. Senter for faithful work done at this time.

In the early part of 1873 Rev. G. W. Johnston became pastor and served the church one year. Rev. M. O. Bailey succeeded in a one-year pastorate. In 1876 Rev. W. O. Grace was called and served the church very acceptably two years. Rev. G. W. Griffin followed him in a two-years' pastorate. On November 1, 1881, Rev. W. G. Inman became pastor and served until December 31, 1892, a period of eleven years and two months, the longest pastorate in the history of the church. Rev. R. P. Mahon succeeded Dr. Inman, beginning

BAPTIST CHURCH, HUMBOLDT.

REV. LLOYD T. WILSON
(Pastor Baptist Church).

his pastorate on July 1, 1893, and continued with the church until October 1, 1898, when he resigned to accept work in Mexico as a missionary.

During the year 1897 the church erected a beautiful and elegant house of worship, at a cost of nearly fifteen thousand dollars. The present pastor, Rev. Lloyd T. Wilson, entered upon his pastorate January 1, 1899.

During the year 1900 a handsome pastor's home was built, at a cost of over two thousand dollars. The church is one of the most active in the State, along all denominational lines. For the first eight years of the history of the church it seems that its records were lost, and it is almost impossible to find out a great many things that are very important.

The first deacons were Jarrett Perry and his brother, Dr. Albert Perry. B. C. Jarrell and W. H. Dodson united with the church in 1870 and 1872, respectively; they were deacons before coming to Humboldt. The next deacons were John C. Glenn and R. P. Lowe. Later other brethren came into the church as deacons, and others were ordained, among them W. T. Bunn, H. C. Burnett, Dr. G. W. James, Dr. J. Max Willett, J. R. Jarrell, A. R. Dodson, Dr. John T. Crews, J. W. Warmoth, C. A. Douglas, William Seward, H. N. Tharp, and B. F. Jarrell.

The first clerk was perhaps Dr. Albert Perry. W. D Woodruff served the church in this capacity from 1875 to 1882. John C. Glenn was clerk from 1882 to 1886; H. W. Roberts, from 1886 to 1888; T. F. Stubbs, from 1888 to 1890; H. C. Barnett, from 1890 to 1896; A. R. Dodson, from 1896 to 1898; A. W. Senter, from 1898 to 1899. C. T. Jarrell was elected clerk in the latter part of 1899 and is the present incumbent.

The first Sunday school superintendent was probably Jarrett Perry; and then came B. C. Jarrell, who served the church for some ten or more years. John C. Glenn succeeded him and was in office about twelve years.

His successor was John T. Crews, who served about five years, removing to Jackson in 1900. B. F. Jarrell became his successor and is the present incumbent.

During the last five years the church has suffered great loss in her membership by death and removal, many of the most important members dying, among them: W. H. Dodson and wife, B. C. Jarrell and wife, Frank Elliott and wife and mother, Mrs. Mary Holloman, Mrs. Sarah Atkins, J. Max. Willett, J. T. and J. W. Blair, Mrs. J. W. Warmoth, John Gill, Mrs.

METHODIST CHURCH, HUMBOLDT.

George Gill, and others; still, the present membership is perhaps the largest in the history of the church, the total being 205.

The Methodist Church of Humboldt.

The Methodist Church at Humboldt was organized in 1860 by Rev. Nathan Sullivan. The congregation first worshiped in a small vacant store building that stood near the Mobile and Ohio Railroad track, some four or five hundred yards south of the present railroad crossing. The first regular pastor was Rev. R. H. Mahon.

In 1861 the congregation worshiped with other denominations in the basement of the

R. W. HOOD
(Pastor Methodist Church).

old Masonic Hall. The church continued to worship here, all the time prospering and adding to its membership, until 1867, when a very good frame church was built on Crenshaw street, which served the congregation for over twenty-three years. During this period the church grew in numbers, influence, and wealth, and in 1899 began the erection of a new brick church, which has just been completed, at a cost of $15,000. This is one of the handsomest churches in the county. The parsonage was built in 1895, costing about $2,000.

The membership of the church is 360; and of the Sunday school, 200.

The present pastor is R. W. Hood. N. A. Senter is superintendent of the Sunday school.

The Cumberland Presbyterian Church of Humboldt.

The Cumberland Presbyterian Church of Humboldt is one of the oldest church organizations in the city. The congregation was organized at old Hopewell Church, a short distance northeast of town, back in the sixties.

The first church built by the congregation was sold to the Christian brethren, and the present handsome and convenient building was erected on Main street, in which the congregation has worshiped since. The old Hopewell Church divided, and a portion of the congregation organized a church at Pleasant Hill, erecting a comfortable frame building, which is now a prosperous and growing organization. This church is served by the pastor of the church at Humboldt.

The church at Humboldt, under the pastorate of Rev. Joe McLesky, is a very flourish-

CUMBERLAND PRESBYTERIAN CHURCH, HUMBOLDT.

ing body, exerting a strong influence in the community. It has a large membership both in church and Sunday school.

"Uncle Joe McLesky," as he is affectionately and familiarly called by his neighbors and friends, is pastor of the Cumberland Presbyterian Church at Humboldt. I am glad to number him as one of my valued friends and a gentleman whose society I enjoyed greatly.

He is known all over West Tennessee and is beloved by many and respected by all. He has preached over forty years, and in that time has come to be known by people of

REV. JOE M'LESKY
(Pastor Cumberland Presbyterian Church, Humboldt).

every class and condition throughout the country. He is a man of strong convictions and earnest purpose, devoted to the service of his Master, but inclined to think that everybody ought to join the Cumberland Presbyterian Church in order to be just right. I am not blaming him for his denominational zeal. It indicates his sincerity and deep-seated convictions—essential requisites of a teacher and preacher.

Rev. Joe McLesky was born in Weakley County, Tenn., on January 23, 1832. He knew what work was in his younger days. He has told me some of his experiences in the logging camps and in teaming in early times. Always of a serious and devotional disposition, he turned to the ministry in early manhood. He was licensed to preach the gospel in 1857.

After the Civil War he was called to the pastorate of the Cumberland Presbyterian Church at Dyersburg and served as its pastor from 1866 to 1870. He then went to Humboldt and served as pastor from 1870 to 1879, when he accepted the pastorate of the church at Dyer. In 1890 he was called to his present charge, serving the church at Humboldt and also at Pleasant Hill, a church about three miles east of the city.

Mr. McLesky has been twice married. After the death of his first wife he married Mrs. Sallie Cooper, an estimable widow lady of Gibson County, who, with three children, the result of this union, constitutes his present family. Mrs. McLesky is a lady of fine social qualities, devoted to her husband, and a zealous worker in the church. The daughters, Miss Maunda M. and Miss Callie T., are bright, talented young ladies, popular in the social world of Humboldt; and Jo—little Jo—can be president of the United States if he tries hard enough. This position is in reach of all the boys, you know; but my little friend has the mind and manners that will carry him to a high mark if he improves them rightly. I hope to live to see him President. I am indebted to this Christian family for many acts of kindness and friendly regard while prosecuting my work, and shall ever remember my association with its members as one of the pleasant episodes of life.

I admire the "rough diamond" character of Uncle Joe McLesky as illustrated both in public and private life, and would gladly devote more space to its expression if the limits of this work permitted. I must content myself, however, with only this brief mention of him and his, trusting that the future may present opportunity for a more emphatic expression of my esteem and regard.

The Presbyterian Church of Humboldt.

The Presbyterian Church of Humboldt was organized on January 7, 1866, with twenty-five members, and is a branch from the old Shiloh Church, which once stood four and one-half miles from Humboldt, northward, and was a famous old meetinghouse in its day, especially under the care of the celebrated Dr. Campbell.

This church is located on Webster street and is a substantial, neat brick building, comfortably furnished, and is lighted with electricity.

The pastor of the church is Rev. John G.

Garth, who was reared in Union City and trained for the ministry at Clarksville. He was ordained and installed pastor at Humboldt on July 4, 1895. This is his only

The Catholic Church of Humboldt.

The Catholic Church at Humboldt was organized in the year 1843 by the Dominican missionary, Rev. Louis Orengo. The mem-

REV. JOHN G. GARTH
(Pastor Presbyterian Church).

REV. J. J. BEUCLER
(Pastor of Catholic Church, since transferred).

charge, and he gives to it his entire time. The church has about one hundred members and has a live Sunday school.

bership then was about two hundred. For ten years Father Orengo attended the spiritual wants of this congregation, as well as

The Christian Church of Humboldt.

This denomination has a very prosperous congregation in Humboldt, consisting of about seventy-five members. The Sunday school has an enrollment of thirty-four. The church was organized about 1896. The church building is a very comfortable brick structure, situated on one of the principal streets. Services are held each Lord's day. The pastor is Elder J. L. Haddock.

The Christian Church has, in addition to the congregation at Humboldt, one at Concord, ten miles northeast of Humboldt; one at Deason's Hall, four miles east. Elder J. L. Haddock preaches for all these congregations.

CATHOLIC CHURCH, HUMBOLDT.

many other local points in West Tennessee. Rev. Patrick O'Brien succeeded him, the mission being attended from Jackson, Tenn., for many years.

In 1894 the present incumbent, Rev. J. J. Beucler, was appointed regular pastor of all West Tennessee missions, with headquarters at Humboldt. During Father Beucler's administration many improvements have been made and a fund started to erect a new church. The Catholic membership numbers about seventy-five.

RESIDENCE OF JOHN M. SENTER, FIRE AND LIFE INSURANCE AGENT, HUMBOLDT.

Public Schools of Humboldt.

The public schools of Humboldt are under the management of a Board of Education, composed of some of the most progressive citizens of the place. These gentlemen have an eye to the best practical results in the matter of education. To this end the best teachers available are selected, and every provision as to the accessories of an educational institution are maintained.

The present building is scarcely adequate to the needs of a city like Humboldt, but it is a substantial brick, commodious and well placed.

A movement is on foot to erect another school building in order to meet the wants of the city.

The school is thoroughly graded, and embraces in its curriculum two grades above the statutory course.

The faculty of the institution is composed of Prof. C. P. Jester, principal; Prof. W. S. Hess, first assistant; Prof. G. A. Campbell, second assistant.

Primary and Intermediate Departments: Miss Lula Ing, Mrs. Bettie Senter, Miss Minnie McDowell, Miss Bessie Senter.

Music Teachers: Miss Dora Wayne Harrell, principal; Miss Marien Campbell, assistant.

Humboldt Courier.

The Humboldt Courier is one of the up-to-date papers of West Tennessee. It is ably conducted, high-toned, and devoted to the interests

HUMBOLDT HIGH SCHOOL.

of the people. It is soundly Democratic in politics, recognizing fully the evolution of ideas in this day of changes, but standing for the main principles that underlie the people's government.

Mr. Sam Gilbert, its able and popular editor, is making the paper a strong factor in the progress and development of Humboldt and the county at large.

The Humboldt Law and Chancery Courts

were established in 1869. These courts have jurisdiction over Civil Districts Nos. 1, 2, 3, 4, 16, and 18. The judges are the same as those of the general courts. The officers of these courts are J. B. Stallings, Sheriff; Clerk of Law Court, J. T. Brown; Clerk and Master of Chancery Court, W. N. L. Dunlap; Deputy Clerk and Master, J. M. Harris.

SAM. GILBERT
(Editor and proprietor of Humboldt Courier).

SOME HUMBOLDT PEOPLE.

Neal A. Senter.

Mr. N. A. Senter, the present official head of the municipal government of the city of Humboldt, has been a citizen of Humboldt since 1867. He has held this office and that of Recorder of the city several terms, and has taken a prominent part in promoting the growth and prosperity of the city. In public office Mr. Senter has exemplified the character of a faithful, zealous, and conscientious servant of the people; as a business man he is distinguished for his reliability and the honorable character of his dealings; and as a citizen there is no one more highly respected and esteemed. His cheerful and companionable disposition, together with an engaging frankness of manner, makes him a universal favorite with his friends and acquaintances. In social life he is ready and helpful in all benevolent enterprises, an active worker in the church, an earnest Christian, and a zealous Mason.

Mr. Senter battled for "the lost cause" during the greater part of that struggle, serving in both the infantry and cavalry service of the Confederate States. His last service was as a lieutenant in the cavalry brigade of Gen. N. B. Forrest. He was wounded several times, and at the battle of Shiloh escaped miraculously with five bullet holes through his hat. While he disclaims the appellation of being a reconstructed rebel and has no apologies to make for his espousal of the Southern cause, his acquiescence in the result of the great struggle is hearty and unaffected. He, with others of his compatriots in and around Humboldt who fought with him, now rejoices

NEAL A. SENTER
(Mayor of Humboldt).

in the blessings resulting from a reunited country and takes a noble pride in the achievements of the great republic.

Humboldt may well be proud of her noble mayor.

James Gillen.

In sketching people and things in and about the enterprising little city of Humboldt, I venture to say a few words about my friend, Mr. James Gillen. Although I had

JAMES GILLEN
(Proprietor of the Humboldt Marble Works).

never met Mr. Gillen before I came to Humboldt, such was the urbanity of his manner that he seemed an old acquaintance. My association with him became very pleasant, and I always found him kind, obliging, and entertaining. He has traveled and read much, and his conversation and society was an agreeable experience. Mr. Gillen is indeed a specimen of the old-time gentleman; and Mrs. Gillen, his estimable wife, whom I also met in social life, is a worthy representative of the old-time gentlewoman, modest in deportment, retiring in disposition, and considerate in her bearing toward others. I am glad to number Mr. and Mrs. Gillen among the many friends I learned to esteem in Humboldt.

Mr. Gillen's native country is Ireland, but he is an American by choice and adoption. He has been a citizen of Humboldt for nearly a quarter of a century and has become a part of its business and social make-up. He has built up a large and prosperous business, and with it has established a character for business integrity that makes his name the synonym of reliability.

Mr. Gillen is a strong believer in the present and future prospects of Humboldt as a business and manufacturing center. He is a large stockholder in the Humboldt Cotton Mills and the Merchants' State Bank, of Humboldt, in both of which he is a director.

Hon. W. I. McFarland.

Ike McFarland, as he is commonly called, was born on March 25, 1835, in Crockett County, Tenn. He was the son of Rev. J. W. McFarland, a prominent minister of the Methodist Church. He was educated in the Alamo High School, at Alamo, Tenn., and at Andrew College, Trenton, Tenn. He was a soldier in the Confederate Army, under the famous general, Bedford Forrest. At the close of the war he entered the practice of law and has pursued that profession successfully ever since. He has been for years an active temperance man, and at one time was the Grand Worthy Patriarch of the Sons of Temperance in Tennessee, then a strong or-

HON. W. I. M'FARLAND.

ganization in the State. His services as a public speaker against the drink traffic have been quite extensive.

Mr. McFarland is a Methodist and has for years represented his church at Humboldt in the various district conferences. He has served as delegate to the Annual Conference from year to year almost continually for a generation or more; and in 1886 he was a delegate to the General Conference of the Methodist Episcopal Church, South, held at Richmond, Va. At the last session of the Annual Conference he was elected one of the delegates to the great Southern Missionary Conference, held at New Orleans on April 23-30, 1901. Always ready to help any good cause, he has aided more or less in the construction of churches for all denominations and school buildings of all kinds within his reach, and is a strong believer in teaching and preaching. He takes an interest in politics, is a Democrat, and has often appeared on the stump when requested to do so, but never resorts to personal abuse or vituperation.

He has been three times a member of the Tennessee General Assembly—twice of the House and once of the Senate. Once in the county of his residence he received every vote but two, although opposed by a strong man, and in all his canvasses he received practically all the votes in his own district and the districts around him. He was never defeated before the people; but, seeing nothing to attract, he ceased years ago to seek office.

He is healthy and cheerful, and is still actively engaged in the practice of law. He has represented the Louisville and Nashville Railroad as local attorney for more than thirty years, and has tried perhaps more damage cases than any other living lawyer in the State.

J. N. Lannom.

J. N. Lannom was the oldest child of Green B. and Mary Lannom. He was born in Rutherford County, Tenn., in 1823, where he continued to reside till 1844, when he removed to Gibson County and settled near the old town of Shiloh. He married Sallie Sharp before leaving Rutherford County, and by that union eight children were born. His wife died in 1857, and he remained single the balance of his life. He was identified with the town of Humboldt from the first, and was instrumental in the upbuilding of the town. He was a believer in the future greatness of the town, and to that end his energy and best efforts were given. In connection with Dr.

J. N. LANNOM.

John P. Sharp and W. C. Thurston he was one of the founders of the town, and much of her present success and prosperity can be credited to his energy and foresight. He never spared of his time and means to benefit the town. He gave the land upon which the present town college now stands; he also gave many other lots to churches and factories. All of this was done to build up Humboldt. His death occurred in 1887, at Humboldt.

John C. Gillespie.

John C. Gillespie was the first settler, and the first railroad agent and post-

JOHN C. GILLESPIE
(Pioneer citizen of Humboldt).

master, and also the first merchant in Humboldt. He was born in North Carolina, and came to Gibson County in 1822. He was one of the founders of the Presbyterian Church in Humboldt and was an elder in the church until his death, which occurred in July, 1877. His son, L. K. Gillespie, has been in business in Humboldt since 1865. He is a highly respected citizen and has been an elder in the church for over twenty years.

W. N. L. Dunlap.

W. N. L. Dunlap was born in Gibson County, two and one-half miles north of Humboldt, on October 15, 1843; was brought up on the farm. Esquire Dunlap entered the Confederate Army in the fall of 1861, and served till the battle of Franklin, when he was severely wounded in the shoulder and was disabled for further service. After the war he engaged in farming for a number of years. He was elected magistrate of the

W. N. L. DUNLAP
(Clerk and Master of Humboldt Law Court and Magistrate of the District).

Third Civil District in 1881, and has filled that office since that time. In October, 1888, he was appointed Clerk and Master of the Chancery Court at Humboldt, which position he still holds.

Esquire Dunlap is a member of the Methodist Church and of the Independent Order of Odd Fellows. He was married to Miss Susan Hess, daughter of Maj. J. A. W. Hess, on November 7, 1872, and by that union they have had eight children, five of whom are living—Warner E., Mary G., Anna Kate, Thomas W. S., and Lula.

Esquire Dunlap is one of the most active and influential members of the County Court and is always foremost in every enterprise that is for the upbuilding of the county.

John E. Campbell.

J. E. Campbell, one of the leading citizens of Humboldt, was born in Grainger County, near Rutledge, in 1851, being now fifty years of age. He came to West Tennessee in the fall of 1873, when about twenty-two years

JOHN E. CAMPBELL.
(Member of School Board).

of age. Although without any means, by untiring energy and business tact he has acquired considerable property and controls a representative value of $50,000. He was married in 1879 to Miss Jennie E. Hess, the youngest of eight daughters of Maj. J. A. W. Hess. He began farming in 1881 on a farm three miles north of Humboldt and was very successful, establishing and successfully managing Oakwood stock farm for several years, and shipping Holstein cattle, Jersey Red hogs, and barred Plymouth Rock chickens; in the meantime acquiring a canning factory and saw and grist mill in Humboldt. In 1899 he built his magnificent residence," Fairview." He then moved into town and soon became a lumber dealer and contractor, putting up some of the finest residences and storehouses in the town and surrounding country. He takes an active interest in the affairs of the county, and is a zealous advocate and promoter of progress and development in all the essentials of social and civil improvement. For a number of years he served acceptably as county surveyor.

Mr. Campbell is a staunch member and an elder of the old-school Presbyterian Church, and believes that religion should be uppermost in all things. He has an interesting family, composed of three girls—Marion L., Gabrilla H., and Lillian J.—and three boys—Levi Ross, Zach J., and James Elbert.

Col. C. H. Ferrell.

Humboldt was not much of a town until after the close of the Civil War. The fact that it was situated in a good farming region, and especially that it was situated at the junc-

COL. C. H. FERRELL.
(President of the Merchants' State Bank of Humboldt).

tion of two important railroad systems, made it a promising point for business enterprise. A number of progressive business men were attracted to the place on account of these considerations. Among these was C. H. Ferrell. Mr. Ferrell came to Humboldt in 1866 and entered upon a mercantile career, soon building up a large and profitable trade, and has been closely identified with the interests and growth of the town ever since.

To begin at the beginning of Mr. Ferrell's career in life, he was born in Dyer County, Tenn., on Christmas day, in the year 1837. This was a good day to be born on and was a favorable element in the horoscope of Mr. Ferrell's life. Perhaps he should have been a preacher, but he was not. It may be said of him, however, that no act of his life has ever cast dishonor upon the day of his nativity.

His early life was passed upon a farm. On arriving at manhood he added the milling business to farm pursuits, prosecuting the same for some years. When the war between the States broke out, he enlisted in the Confederate Army, joining the Twelfth Tennessee Infantry. He served in this branch of the service until the latter part of the war, when he entered the cavalry service, under General Forrest.

In 1864, just before the close of the war, he married Miss Lavinia Kelly Scales, an estimable young lady, belonging to a prominent

MRS. C. H. FERRELL.

family of Gibson County. We have seen that he came to Humboldt and began merchandising in 1866, soon after the close of the war. He continued this business until 1872, in the meantime and in the years following acquiring considerable land interests and also becoming interested in farming enterprises of a varied nature.

In 1874 he organized and established a large nursery plant, which developed into a very extensive and highly profitable business. This business he prosecuted for fourteen years, with great profit. He closed out his nursery business in 1888. Previous to this, in 1887, he, with others, organized the Farmers and Merchants' Bank of Humboldt, becoming its president. In 1893 this bank was consolidated with another institution of Humboldt, the Tennessee State Bank, forming the present Merchants' State Bank, of which Mr. Ferrell became president, occupying this position down to the present time.

Mr. Ferrell has been an active business man and promoter of business enterprises in Humboldt ever since he adopted it as his home. In addition to his position as president of the local bank, he is also president of the McNairy County Bank, at Selmer, McNairy County, which is a branch of the Merchants' State Bank of Humboldt.

Colonel Ferrell's activity in the promotion of useful enterprises in Humboldt is illustrated in the part he took in the organization and capitalization of the Humboldt Cotton Mills, an institution that contributes greatly to the upbuilding of Humboldt and furnishes employment to many of its people. He is a large stockholder and vice president of this large industry.

Mr. Ferrell is a ready and helpful participant in all movements to improve and better the religious, moral, and educational interests of the community, giving liberally of his time and means in support of these interests. He was the largest contributor to the building and furnishing of the new Methodist Church in Humboldt, a structure that will compare favorably in architectural beauty with any in the State. He is a member of this church and also one of its trustees, and in his daily walk and conversation exemplifies the character of a Christian gentleman and an upright citizen.

J. B. Stallings.

Mr. Stallings came of good old North Carolina stock, his father having settled in Gibson County in 1833. He was born on November 19, 1857, on a farm about four miles northwest of Humboldt, and has lived on a farm all of his life. His present business is that of farming, devoting special attention to the raising of small fruits and vegetables for the Northern markets, and as deputy sheriff of the county. As deputy sheriff his special duty is to serve as the executive officer of the Humboldt Law

J. B. STALLINGS
(Prominent farmer and Deputy Sheriff of Gibson County).

and Chancery Court. Mr. Stallings served four years as deputy during the terms of Sheriff B. F. Jones, and is the present incumbent as deputy under R. E. Morgan, the present sheriff of the county. His personal worth and ability is recognized by the community in which he lives by their entrusting him with various public duties. He is now and has been for several years one of the school directors of the Third Civil District, and was for a number of years supervisor of roads in the same district.

Mr. Stallings is noted for his hospitality and liberality; and his beautiful country home, presided over by his noble wife, is always a most delightful place to stop.

He is known throughout his surrounding community as the big-hearted, jovial Jim B.

Stallings. He has been married twice, and by the first union several children were born, only one of which is living—a son, Walter.

J. J. Thweatt.

Mr. John J. Thweatt is a native of Dinwiddie County, Va. He came to Tennessee when a mere lad and attended the public schools of Memphis, prosecuting his studies under his brother, Prof. Noble Thweatt.

J. J. THWEATT.

While yet young he entered the dry goods business as a clerk, and for some years was in the employ of B. Lowenstein Bros., of Memphis. After the yellow fever epidemic of 1878 he made Humboldt his home, embarking in the dry goods business. His push and energy soon placed him among the leading merchants of the city of Humboldt, and for many years his establishment was one of the largest and most popular in the place.

In 1882 Mr. Thweatt married Miss Cora L. Fox, daughter of the late Dr. W. L. Fox, of Humboldt. Four children—three boys and one girl—have blessed this union.

After a long and successful business career, Mr. Thweatt's health became impaired; and selling out his business he organized the Humboldt Mercantile Company, becoming its president. This position gave him time for recuperation and attention to his outside affairs.

It may be truthfully said that few men in Humboldt have done more to upbuild the town than Mr. Thweatt. He has given liberally of his time and means to promote the industries of the town and build up the churches and schools. He has been active in building up the banking institutions of the place. He was vice president of the old Farmers and Merchants' Bank, and was on the committee consolidating that institution with the Tennessee State Bank, forming the present Merchants' State Bank of Humboldt, of which he is now director.

Mr. Thweatt's citizenship is of such character that he may be said to be one of the pillars of the social well-being of his town; active and helpful in church and Sunday school and in all movements for the public good. He is a member of and an elder in the Cumberland Presbyterian Church.

J. J. R. Adams.

J. J. R. Adams, a prominent merchant and business man of the town of Humboldt, is a native of McNairy County, Tenn. He came to Gibson County in 1867 and located at

J. J. R. ADAMS
(A leading merchant of Humboldt).

Humboldt, engaging in the manufacture of shingles, which he prosecuted with good success for several years.

In 1870 he entered the mercantile business in Humboldt, dealing in family groceries and

hardware, in which business he has continued since, covering a business career of thirty-one years. During this time Mr. Adams has displayed and illustrated the virtues that enter into the character and life of a successful business man and useful citizen. His business career has been successful to the extent of accumulating a comfortable estate, and his course as a citizen has been such as to merit and receive the respect and esteem of his fellow citizens. Prompt and honorable in business affairs, he has been equally mindful of his social obligations, giving his encouragement and influence to all measures and movements intended for the good of the community.

Mr. Adams was for a number of years one of the Board of Aldermen of the town of Humboldt, and served as treasurer of the corporation. He is a consistent and valued member of the Methodist Church, South, and also of the order of Odd Fellows, besides belonging to several other benevolent organizations.

John M. Senter.

Mr. John M. Senter, whose photogravure is given here, is one of the rising young business men of Humboldt. He was born in Humboldt on September 21, 1868, and has always made Humboldt his home. His steadiness of character and practical business qualities have kept him in responsible positions ever since attaining manhood. He was for twelve or fifteen years connected with some of the leading dry goods houses of Humboldt in the capacity of general salesman, eleven years of the time being spent with the popular and enterprising establishment of J. J. Thweatt.

On December 26, 1895, he married Miss Mattie Tinsley, an estimable young lady of Humboldt; and two years thereafter, in September, 1897, he resigned his position with Mr. Thweatt and entered the general insurance business. Since that time he has devoted himself to the latter pursuit and has built up the largest insurance business in the city of Humboldt.

His business covers all classes of risks—fire, life, accident, tornado, plate glass, steam boiler, employers' liability, health, etc. Some of the largest and most reliable fire insurance companies in the world are represented in his office—notably, the Royal, of Liverpool; North British and Mercantile; Ætna, of Hartford; New York Underwriters;

JOHN M. SENTER
(Prominent insurance agent).

Westchester, of New York; Greenwich, of New York; American Central, of St. Louis; and the Home, of New York, the last making a specialty of farm risks. The Union Central Life Insurance Company, of Cincinnati, a strong and progressive life company, does a large business in his agency. He also represents the American Casualty Company, writing accident, plate glass, boiler, employers' liability, and health insurance.

The aggregate insurance capital represented in Mr. Senter's office is more than one hundred million dollars.

Besides being a strong factor in the business life of Humboldt, Mr. Senter's usefulness as a citizen is universally felt and recognized. He is prominent and active in the cause of religion and education and in his support of measures and movements for the general good. He is a member of the Methodist Church, South, and of the Masonic fraternity, being secretary of Humboldt Lodge.

John W. Gatewood.

John W. Gatewood, freight agent of the Louisville and Nashville Railroad, is a native of Mississippi and is a descendant of one of the oldest and best families in the South. He was born in 1852 in Scott County, and was educated at the Somerville (Miss.) High School.

In 1882 he came to Humboldt and accepted a position with the Louisville and Nashville

JOHN W. GATEWOOD.
(Agent of the Louisville & Nashville Railroad, Humboldt).

Railroad, and has been in the service of this road in various capacities ever since. He was promoted at different times until he arose to the position which he now fills with credit to himself and the Louisville and Nashville Railroad Company.

Mr. Gatewood not only takes high rank as a practical railroad man, but is a most popular and enterprising citizen. He was for several terms elected a member of the City Council, which was an evidence of the esteem in which he is held by our people. In his official capacity he always had the interests of the city at heart, and worked for the advancement of every enterprise that would add to the growth and prosperity of Humboldt.

Mr. Gatewood was married in 1884 to Miss Laura Belle Watkins, and has an interesting family. He is a quiet, kind-hearted gentleman of the old Southern type, and has friends among all classes. He is one of the most efficient and popular men the Louisville and Nashville Railroad ever had at Humboldt.

I. H. Dungan.

I. H. Dungan, one of the most popular and enterprising citizens of the city of Humboldt, was born in Hardin County, Tenn., on May 24, 1855. He came to Humboldt when quite a youth and resided with Hon. W. I. McFarland, a cousin by marriage, who sent him to school for four years. He then entered the retail grocery trade, forming a partnership under the name of Fox, Hamilton & Dungan. The firm was burned out in 1882 by a disastrous fire, which swept away thirty-one business houses, the firm losing everything. With undaunted pluck, Mr. Dungan set up business again on his own account and prosecuted the same with splendid success until 1890, when he was again the victim of the fire fiend, losing heavily by a second fire.

In 1893 he was appointed postmaster at Humboldt, serving five years. In 1897 he established the Humboldt Hoop and Heading

I. H. DUNGAN.

Factory, now one of the chief industries of the city. Mr. Dungan is noted for his enterprise and public spirit. He has been the active spirit in securing for the city some of its leading enterprises—notably, the Bank of Humboldt, the Commercial Hotel, and a stave factory and flouring mill. He is still untiring in his efforts to induce capital and manufacturing enterprises to locate in Humboldt.

He married Miss Willie Fox, the accomplished daughter of Dr. W. L. Fox, deceased, and finds in the married state the supreme happiness of life.

J. A. Collinsworth.

John Aladdin Collinsworth was born on a farm near the city of Humboldt, Tenn., on January 23, 1872. He was educated in the common schools of the neighborhood, supplemented by several years' attendance at the

J. A. COLLINSWORTH
(Attorney).

Jackson High School, at Henderson, and also in the schools of Nashville. He took a special business course in the Humboldt Business College.

In 1893 he entered the Law School of Cumberland University, at Lebanon, Tenn., graduating therefrom with honors. He began the practice of law at Somerville, Tenn., soon after his graduation and was meeting with splendid success when, being offered a partnership with Hon. G. W. Wade, a distinguished lawyer of his native county, he removed to his old home of Humboldt and entered the practice there. This firm prospered during its continuance, but in 1896 Mr. Wade withdrew to enter politics. Since that time Ladd, as he is familiarly known, has continued the practice, building up a fine business. Soon after his location in Humboldt he was elected one of its Aldermen, serving also as secretary of the board and chairman of the finance committee. While filling these offices the new water and light plants of the city were put into successful operation.

In 1897 he was elected Mayor of the city, serving in that office two years, declining a reëlection on account of the exigencies of his law practice. He made an excellent record as Mayor and in all the offices he held, demonstrating his zeal in the public service and fitness for public trust.

He now has a large and increasing law practice, and is one of the rising young men of Gibson County. He is a member and active worker in a number of the benevolent orders, and also a member of the Methodist Episcopal Church, South, at Humboldt, and a zealous participant in church and Sunday school work.

Mr. Collinsworth is a young man of most exemplary habits, and possesses a high sense of honor and devotion to moral principles. He is still unmarried.

A. R. DODSON
(Cashier Merchants' State Bank).

A. R. Dodson.

A. R. Dodson, cashier of the Merchants' State Bank of Humboldt, was born in Gibson County in 1865, and came with his parents to Humboldt in 1872. He is a graduate of the Southwestern Baptist University, at Jackson, Tenn., receiving the B. A. degree in that institution. He completed his business course at Eastman's Business College, Poughkeepsie, N. Y., in October, 1886, in his twenty-first year.

He was elected cashier of the Farmers and Merchants' Bank of Humboldt, and when that bank consolidated with the Tennessee State Bank, forming the Merchants' State Bank, he was elected cashier of the latter, which position he has filled down to the present time. Mr. Dodson's business career has been spent entirely in Humboldt, although offered many tempting inducements elsewhere in the banking business. Having been associated with Mr. C. H. Ferrel for fourteen years in a successful prosecution of the banking business, he feels reluctant to break old ties or sever the bonds that link him to the friends and associates of his home city.

RESIDENCE OF J. J. SNYDER, HUMBOLDT.

MANUFACTORIES AND BUSINESS ENTERPRISES.

B. C. Jarrell & Co., Manufacturers of Fruit Packages.

The history of the firm of B. C. Jarrell & Co. dates from 1870. In that year Mr. B. C. Jarrell moved from Wilson County, Tenn., and in partnership with Col. James Hamilton, of Lebanon, Tenn., erected a small sawmill, about four miles west of Humboldt, Mr. Jarrell having the active management of the business. This mill was moved to Humboldt in 1879, at which time a small planing machine was added.

On January 20, 1880, the firm known as the Humboldt Buggy and Wagon Company began operations. This firm was composed of B. C. Jarrell, James Hamilton, Dr. J. E. D. Scott, and J. W. Philp, and was formed for the purpose of manufacturing high-grade wagons and buggies, of which a large number were made while this branch of the business was prosecuted.

In 1883 the manufacture of fruit packages was begun in a small way. This branch of the business was increased gradually from year to year until 1887, when the firm was reorganized, the interest of J. W. Philp and and Dr. J. E. D. Scott (then deceased) being purchased by Jarrell and Hamilton; and J. R. Jarrell and B. F. Jarrell, sons of B. C. Jarrell, were made members of the firm.

Buggies and wagons were manufactured in a limited way for three or four years by the reorganized firm, when this branch of the business was discontinued.

On October 1, 1890, the interest of Col. James Hamilton was purchased and C. T. Jarrell was admitted, the firm then consisting of B. C. Jarrell and three sons, J. R., B. F., and C. T. Jarrell.

B. C. Jarrell continued at the head of the

MANUFACTURING PLANT OF B. C. JARRELL & CO.

firm until his death. After the death of Mr. Jarrell, his interest remained in the business until September 1, 1900, when J. R. Jarrell, B. F. Jarrell, and C. T. Jarrell became sole proprietors, operating the business under the old firm name of B. C. Jarrell & Co.

The demand for building material and fruit packages of all kinds, especially the latter, has increased to such an extent that the manufactory now is one of the largest in West Tennessee, and its product is shipped to many of the States of the Union. The machinery and buildings for carrying on the work cover a large area of ground and the establishment gives employment to a vast force. The manufactory has its own electric light plant and every appliance for the work, both in the latest improved machinery and commodious buildings and warehouses for the storage of finished product.

B. C. Jarrell, the founder of the B. C. Jarrell plant, was born on a farm in Wilson County, Tenn., near the town of Lebanon, on February 5, 1836. He left the farm on attaining manhood and engaged in the milling business in his native county, prosecuting the same until his removal to Gibson County in 1870. His career in business in Gibson County was continually successful, being marked by unusual correctness of judgment and industry. In public life he was esteemed for his usefulness and in private life beloved for his virtues. An epitome of his character may be embraced in a few words. He was enterprising, prompt, and honorable in business affairs; and in his social relations he exemplified the character and fulfilled the duties of a sincere Christian gentleman. He died, universally regretted by his fellow citizens, on April 6, 1900.

B. C. JARRELL.

Dodson Plow Company—Biographical Sketch of W. H. Dodson.

W. H. Dodson was born in Halifax County, Va., on June 8, 1815. He was the second son of William T. and Sallie (Young) Dodson, both native Virginians. His father was a farmer and mechanic; was married in 1811, but came with his family from his native State to Davidson County, Tenn., in 1823 and died in 1832, preceded by his wife several years. Of the nine children, five lived to be grown.

W. H. Dodson was about eight years of age when he came to Tennessee, and was left an orphan at seventeen. He attended school only about six weeks after he attained youthful age; however, by his own efforts he acquired a very good practical education. Being thus thrown upon his own resources at an early age, he began work on the river, working on a keel, flat, and steamboat. In 1836 he steered a flat from Nashville to New Orleans, continuing to follow boating for several years on the Tennessee, Cumberland, Forked Deer, Yalabusha, Yazoo, Tallahatchie, and Big Black Rivers. By his frugality he saved some money and began trading in stock and poultry from Nashville to New Orleans.

In 1841 he moved from Nashville to West Tennessee and settled in Eaton, Gibson County, becoming engaged in the family grocery business, boating on the Forked Deer River, and trading in New Orleans. In 1846 he associated himself with James A. Harwood, adding dry goods to the business. In this relationship he continued for three years, at the close of which time he sold out to Mr. Harwood. He then engaged in farming, sawmilling, and the stock business, in which business he continued until the breaking out of the Civil War. After this he returned to Eaton and again resumed general merchandise business, in company with his son-in-law, J. R. Dance. After two years Mr. Dance retired from the business and Mr. T. C. Pat-

DODSON PLOW WORKS.

terson was admitted as a partner; but in 1870 the firm of Dodson & Patterson was dissolved, the former retiring, and the business was continued by Patterson & Bros. With this the subject of our sketch closed his career in

W. H. DODSON.

the general merchandise business, and in 1871 moved to Trenton, Tenn., but remained there only a short time.

Coming to Humboldt in the year 1872, Mr. Dodson purchased a one-half interest in the plow factory and foundry of William Jarrell, at the same place, the latter gentleman being the inventor and owner of the celebrated Jarrell plow, cotton scraper and planter, known throughout the South and West. The first year they added a flouring mill to the other business. This business relation continued to 1878, when Mr. Dodson purchased the entire interest of Mr. Jarrell and continued the business in his own name, assisted in the management by his son, C. J. Dodson. On September 1, 1895, the firm was again changed, the new firm being styled "The Dodson Plow Company," Mr. C. J. Dodson being admitted as a partner. Mr. Dodson did the principal traveling for the different firms for twenty-seven years. Notwithstanding the fact that he was actively engaged in the manufacturing business all these years, he was very public-spirited along other lines.

In 1887 he and others organized and established the Farmers and Merchants' Bank of Humboldt, his son, Mr. A. R. Dodson being elected cashier.

In 1889 he also organized and established the Haywood County Bank, of Brownsville, Tenn., his son, W. W. Dodson, being elected assistant cashier.

In 1893 Mr. Dodson and Mr. E. A. Collins organized and established the Milan Banking Company, of Milan, Tenn., his son, L. P. Dodson, being elected assistant cashier.

In 1895 he organized and established the Farmers and Merchants' Bank, of Dyer, Tenn., his grandson, Russell Dance, being elected cashier.

On January 9, 1843, Mr. Dodson married Sarah T. Morton, who died on August 16 of the same year. On June 17, 1847, he wedded J. A. Blakemore, daughter of W. T. and Jane R. Blakemore, and of ten children born to them five are yet living, viz: W. W., Ida (Mrs. W. H. Gregory), C. J., A. R., and L. P. Dodson.

In May, 1897, Mr. Dodson made a visit to his old home in Brooklyn, Halifax County, Va., returning after an absence of seventy-five years; but he could find no one living in the little village who was as old as he, or could tell him anything about the village of his boyhood days, and there was nothing left by which he could trace where the "old home" used to stand.

On June 17, 1897, Mr. and Mrs. Dodson celebrated their fiftieth anniversary, or golden wedding, on which occasion their children, grandchildren, and quite a number of their old friends were present.

On August 8, 1898, death came to the once happy home and took from it his lifelong companion and dearly beloved wife. Mr. Dodson was a man of strong constitution and enjoyed exceptionally good health until after the death of his wife, when his health began to fail. He died on February 2, 1901, rich and ripe in many graces.

Mr. Dodson was a Democrat and a Mason, and he and his wife were for many years very active and devoted members of the Missionary Baptist Church, the former being senior deacon of the church at Humboldt, Tenn., at the time of his death. He was liberal with his means and always willing to help those in distress, and never turned away any who asked him for help without giving. In business affairs he was always willing to help those who were worthy and striving to help themselves. He commenced life without a penny, and yet by honest and hard work accumulated quite a fortune. He assisted very largely with his means in building the handsome First Baptist Church at this place in 1897, and also the beautiful parsonage erected in the fall of 1900, and was a liberal contributor to all the calls of his church.

C. J. DODSON
(Of Dodson Plow Company).

Mr. C. J. Dodson, the present owner and operator of the Dodson Plow Company, is a native of West Tennessee. He was educated in I. O. O. F. College, Humboldt; University of Tennessee, Knoxville; and Eastman Business College, Poughkeepsie, N. Y.; and he is a man of considerable experience, having been engaged in active business since about 1880. He is a very practical man, having been engaged in the wholesale business in Memphis for a short while, and for many years associated with his father in the manufacturing business, having had the management of his large manufacturing interest since 1895 and been a partner with him from that time until his death, since which time he has been sole owner of the Dodson Plow Company. His firm is one of the best known in this section, doing an extensive business in the South and West. His company is the sole manufacturer of the Jarrell cast plows and cotton scrapers; they also make a line of chilled plows and enjoy a large trade, especially throughout Tennessee, Arkansas, Mississippi, Louisiana, Missouri, Alabama, and Texas.

The Humboldt Cotton Mills.

This is the largest manufacturing establishment in Gibson County. It is situated just outside the corporate limits of the city of Humboldt and covers, with its tenements for employees, an area of fourteen acres of ground. The mills are operated by a stock company, incorporated under the general laws of the State, the stockholders being citizens of Humboldt and vicinity. The organization was effected in May, 1900, with an authorized capital of $100,000. The plant consists of a main factory building 125 feet wide by 206 feet in length, one story high; separate boiler and engine rooms, with capacity for doubling power of plant; standard warehouse 40x100 feet, all brick. The power consists of a Lane & Bodley Columbian Corless Engine of 200-horse power, made with provision for an additional cylinder and boiler to increase power to 400-horse. For the convenience of employees there are upon the factory grounds fifteen four-room and ten two-room cottages—all bright, clean, and comfortable.

The entire operating equipment of the mills is of the newest pattern in every department. The plant has a capacity for 15,000 spindles and 400 looms. At present 4,000 spindles and 100 looms are in operation, using 2,000 bales of cotton per annum and giving employment to 100 operatives.

The mill has its own electric lighting and water supply system, the former consisting of a 30 K. W. generator and the latter of a 300-foot well, with a force pump and an 80,000-gallon reservoir on the south wall of the main building.

Every modern appliance for the extinguish-

HUMBOLDT COTTON MILLS.

ment of fire is provided, embracing a powerful force pump, automatic sprinklers, and hose reaching every part of the plant.

The special goods manufactured are four-yard sheetings of a grade and quality that have already secured a high standing in the market, though its looms were but recently started.

The officers of the institution are: H. C. Burnett, president; C. H. Ferrell, vice president; R. L. Beare, secretary; A. R. Dodson, treasurer. Directors: H. C. Burnett, C. H. Ferrell, R. L. Beare, A. R. Dodson, J. R. Jarrell, James Gillen, and W. W. Baird. T. H. Lever is superintendent.

Humboldt Marble Works.

The cut given shows the carving department of the Humboldt Marble Works, one of the thriving industries of this progressive city. These works have been in operation for almost a quarter of a century and have an established trade throughout the South and

INTERIOR VIEW OF HUMBOLDT MARBLE WORKS.

Southwest. Mr. James Gillen, who owns and operates the works, has a thorough knowledge of the business, having served at the trade for several years before establishing his present factory.

The reputation of the Humboldt Marble Works for painstaking and promptitude in the execution of orders, acquired by many years of strict business attention, has contributed largely to the extent and volume of its business. The industry is an important feature of Humboldt's manufacturing interests. It gives employment to about thirty skilled workmen, at good wages. The pay roll of the establishment amounts to upwards of $300 per week. I am informed by representatives of the two railroads serving Humboldt that the freight charges on material—raw and finished—delivered to and from this factory is a principal item in the railroad business of the city.

Humboldt Spoke Factory.

Frank X. Foltz, proprietor of the Humboldt Spoke Factory, is a native of Indiana, and was born on a farm near Madison, in Ripley County. After the death of his father and division of his estate, Mr. Foltz concluded he would change his business, and went to work in a livery stable; then he learned the spoke business, and moved with Weis & Sons to Union City, Tenn. After

FRANK X. FOLTZ.

leaving Union City he came with Beck & Gardner to Humboldt and worked with them until they sold their factory to the American Wheel Company. He then acted as foreman for this company until their plant was burned down in 1891. Mr. Foltz then started a fac-

HUMBOLDT SPOKE WORKS.

tory of his own, which he has successfully operated since. The capacity of his factory is 7,000 spokes per day. Material is obtained along the Louisville and Nashville and the Mobile and Ohio Railroads and by wagon transportation. The products of this factory are marketed in Illinois, Michigan, Ohio, South Carolina, Canada, and, in fact, all over the world. He manufactures all kinds and sizes of oak and hickory spokes, plain wood hub, Sarven patent and shell hand, finished and complete.

Mr. Foltz is a prominent and highly esteemed citizen. He is a man of push and enterprise, and is always for everything that will advance the interests of his town.

Humboldt Hoop and Heading Company.

This important woodworking industry was established in 1898 by Mr. I. H. Dungan. In 1901 he took in as a partner Mr. W. H. Shimwell, of Erin, Tenn. The firm is engaged in the manufacture of coiled elm hoops and slack barrel heading. They also operate a sawmill in connection with their other business. The output of the plant in 1900 was 300,000 sets of heading, 1,500,000 hoops, and 1,500,000 feet of lumber, involving a value of over $30,000. The output of the current year will exceed this. They employ in the various departments of the business some forty or more people.

W. H. SHIMWELL.

Mr. W. H. Shimwell, one of the proprietors of the Humboldt Hoop and Heading Company, was born in Stewart County in 1864. At an early age his parents moved to Erin, Houston, County, where he was educated. On arriving at manhood he engaged in the woodworking business, manufacturing staves, heading, etc., which he has followed for fifteen years. In 1887 he married Miss Julia McMillin, of Erin, by which union he has three children. He moved to Humboldt in 1897, and for two years engaged in the mercantile business. In the beginning of the present year he sold out his mercantile business and became a partner with Mr. I. H. Dungan in the operation of the Humboldt Hoop and Heading Factory.

Mr. Shimwell is a zealous member of the Cumberland Presbyterian Church of Humboldt, and also of the Masonic and Odd Fellow fraternities of the same place. He is highly esteemed in both business and social circles.

Humboldt Ice Factory and Bottling Works.

This plant was established in 1890 by Robert Beare, Taylor Beare, and William Beare, and operated by them under the firm name of Beare Bros. This is one of the prosperous manufactories of Humboldt.

The product of the factory is marketed throughout the county and along the lines of

BEARE BROS.' ICE FACTORY AND BOTTLING PLANT

the Louisville and Nashville and the Mobile and Ohio Railroads in adjoining sections. The product of the factory bears a special reputation for purity and quality. The refrigerating capacity is twenty-five tons; cold storage capacity, seven hundred tons.

The firm has recently organized the Humboldt Bottling Works, manufacturing soda pop and other bottled goods as an addition to their business. These goods are coming into general use in the country, supplanting other manufactures on account of their excellent quality.

The Beare brothers are descended from old Virginia stock and stand high in the business and social life of Humboldt.

Eclipse Marble Works.

This business was established in 1882 by the present owner, Mr. A. H. Stehr, who is a practical man and who has built up an extensive business, extending over the States of Mississippi, Tennessee, Louisiana, Arkansas, Texas, and parts of other States. Among the very fine pieces of work that he has turned out is that very large granite shaft in the Brownsville cemetery, to the memory of Captain Phillips; one at Milan for Mr. Webb Adams; a large mausoleum at LaFayette, La.; the Professor McGee monument at Trenton; the Ward monument at Greenfield, Tenn.; and the very handsome Nussbaum mausoleum at Cape Girardeau, Mo.

E. W. Ing & Sons.

An important industry in Humboldt is the flouring and grist mill operated in the name of E. W. Ing & Sons. This mill was estab-

E. W. ING.

lished about 1885. It has a capacity of forty barrels per day, and is equipped with modern process machinery. The product of the mill is of fine quality and is mainly consumed by the home market. The firm at

ECLIPSE MARBLE WORKS; A. H STEHR, PROPRIETOR.

present is composed of E. W. Ing, Jr., W. C. Ing, and J. M. Ing, all natives of Gibson County. Their father, E. W. Ing, Sr., whose picture is here presented, was the original owner and operator of the plant; he died in 1897. Mr. E. W. Ing, Sr., was one of the pioneer citizens of Gibson County, having lived in and near Humboldt the greater part of his life, and saw it grow from a village of a few inhabitants to a thriving town of twenty-five hundred people. He was twice mayor of Humboldt, and at his death was one of the magistrates of the municipality. He was a member of the Methodist Church, South, and also of the Masonic fraternity, and a highly useful and respected citizen of the community in which his life was spent. After his death his sons continued the business he had established. Mr. E. W. Ing, Jr., is the manager of the business, devoting his entire attention to the same. J. M. Ing is in the service of the Louisville and Nashville Railroad, with headquarters at Paris, Tenn.; and W. C. Ing is a conductor on one of the through freight trains of the same road. They all regard Humboldt as their home.

Merchants' State Bank, of Humboldt.

This bank was formed by the consolidation of the Farmers and Merchants' Bank and the Tennessee State Bank, in February, 1894. The Farmers and Merchants' Bank was organized in May, 1887, with paid in capital of $12,500; Mr. C. H. Ferrell was president and Mr. A. R. Dodson was cashier. During the existence of this bank Mr. M. T. Cox was vice president, and at his death Mr. J. J. Thweatt was elected as his successor.

From the beginning the bank was a success and was prominent among the financial institutions of the State for conservative management. The growing business necessitated additional capital, and the paid-up capital was increased to $33,000. An ample surplus fund was laid aside to meet contingencies.

The Tennessee State Bank was organized in 1890, with Mr. R. E. Gardner as president; Mr. O. C. Sharp, vice president; and Mr. J. R. Jarrell, cashier; having a capital of $50,000. In 1892 Mr. R. E. Gardner resigned the presidency, and Mr. W. H. Bobbitt was elected his successor.

This bank was the outgrowth of the business prosperity Humboldt was then enjoying. The popularity of its officers gave it a reputation second to none in the State, and it enjoyed the confidence of the business community. This bank, with the Farmers and Merchants' Bank, successfully passed the panic of 1893. The stockholders of both banks deciding that better dividends could be realized from uniting the two banks, voted to consolidate in February, 1894.

MERCHANTS' STATE BANK.

The Merchants' State Bank now has over $80,000 capital and surplus, and ranks among the foremost institutions of the State. It has more than returned to stockholders its capital in dividends and surplus since organization. It has over sixty stockholders, and its directory consists of some of the most prominent business men and farmers of the county. Its directors have always fostered every enterprise that had for its purpose the upbuilding of the town. It bought at par the $15,000 in six per cent bonds issued for the city water works and electric light plant, and has held them as an investment, besides carrying a large floating debt for the city.

The Humboldt Cotton Mills is one of the more recent enterprises which has been built principally by the stockholders of this bank. Mr. J. R. Adams has successfully managed a branch bank for this institution at Selmer, Tenn.

Bank of Humboldt.

This institution is one of the comparatively new enterprises of the city of Humboldt, brought about by the growing volume of business and increasing demand for business capital in this progressive little city.

The bank was organized and incorporated in 1899 under the general banking laws of the State, and immediately secured most satisfactory recognition from the business public. Its promoters were all men of tried business standing and responsibility. Since its establishment the bank has continued to grow in public favor and is now receiving a good share of the business of the community. It has a handsome building on the principal street of the town, the latest improved fire and burglar proof safes. The offices are spacious and well-arranged.

The officers of the bank are men of fine business ability and courteous manners. J. H. Thomas occupies the position of president; G. W. Bailey, that of vice president; and C. H. Fox, that of bookkeeper. The directory consists of G. W. Bailey, O. C. Sharp, W. M. Hamilton, J. H. Hamilton, John S. Lewis, J. H. Thomas, L. E. Humphries, E. W. Ing, F. X. Foltz, J. W. Warmath, W. T. Williams, E. L. Fox, and S. G. Scruggs.

The last statement of the condition of the bank, made on December 31, 1900, shows the prosperous condition of this institution. It held in secured loans and discounts $68,366.72; cash, $25,380.32—making its total available assets $93,747.04. Its liability to depositors and bills payable aggregated $68,277.96; making its surplus as to depositors $25,470.08. The statement shows a very substantial accumulation of undivided profits arising from its less than two years' business, besides paying a satisfactory dividend to its stockholders.

Humboldt School for Colored Children.

This is one of the largest and most prosperous schools for colored children in the

BANK OF HUMBOLDT.

county. The school is managed by the Board of Education of the city, and has an enrollment of two hundred and fifty pupils.

Prof. T. M. Stigall, the principal of the Humboldt Colored School, was educated at Central Tennessee College, Nashville. He first taught in the public schools of Tipton, Tenn., and afterwards in Madison and Gibson

Counties, proving himself to be a most competent and successful educator of his race. He was elected principal of the Humboldt school in 1897.

PROF. T. M. STIGALL.

Mr. Stigall is a man of fine presence and great natural ability, which, with his excellent scholastic training, fits him peculiarly for the position he occupies. Both he and his wife are very highly respected by the people of Humboldt.

MRS. E. O. STIGALL.

Mrs. E. O. Stigall, assistant principal of the Humboldt Colored School, was educated at Hartshorn Memorial College, Richmond, Va., where she graduated in 1888. She began teaching at Blakesburgh, Va., where she taught one session. She then came to Humboldt in 1890, teaching in the public schools of the city four years. She then resigned and went to Virginia, teaching one session at the Christianburg Industrial Institute. She then returned to Humboldt in 1896, teaching there since.

The school conducted by Professor and Mrs. Stigall is gaining quite a reputation and has turned out two very competent teachers in the colored schools of the county.

Mrs. Stigall is a woman of fine attainments and much general knowledge. She is well read and has the interests of the colored race at heart.

Humboldt Business Directory.

Agricultural Implements and Hardware.—W. H. Lile, A. Y. Simmons, Hudson & Allison, J. J. R. Adams, J. C. Byars, W. E. Dunlap.

Bakers and Confectioners.—E. Honshell, Lanier & Dance, A. Koelz.

Blacksmiths.—Hudson & Allison.

Brick Manufacturers.—W. H. McKnight, J. C. Haley.

Banks.—Merchants' State Bank, Bank of Humboldt.

Barbers.—George Hethcock, Anthony Ragen (colored).

Dry Goods, Clothing, etc.—Liles & Snyder, B. F. McFarland, O. C. Sharp, Humboldt Dry Goods Company, J. Baum, T. A. Bond, B. Learned, Rooks & Wilkinson, B. L. Isaacs.

Dairies.—Geo. Williams.

Drugs.—W. R. Watkins, A. Thweatt, J. F. Parsons, W. H. Mason.

Dentists.—J. W. Thompson, R. F. Green.

Fruits and Vegetables.—P. T. Church.

Furniture and Stoves.—Graham & Johnson, Humboldt Mercantile Co.

Groceries.—W. E. Hale & Son, Lanier & Dance, W. A. Duffy, J. J. R. Adams, C. E. Williams, W. N. Chunn, Humboldt Mercantile Company, T. P. Bethshears, N. A. Senter & Son, H. P. James, F. T. Cates, D. Donovan, H. B. Roe, S. Boykin, John Sheppard.

Hotels.—Commercial (Brooks Long, proprietor), Donovan, Central.

Insurance.—John M. Senter, J. W. Mathis, A. R. Dodson, E. L. Fox.

Jewelers.—Beare Bros., B. Wilkerson.

Liverymen.—F. M. Newhouse & Son, Clark & Warmoth.

Lawyers.—W. I. McFarland, W. H. Bobbitt, J. D. Senter, W. M. McCall, John S. Lewis, John A. Collinsworth.

Milliners.—Miss E. E. Moore, O. C. Sharp.

Meat Markets.—Hamilton & Haralson, T. D. Saunders, Tucker.

Printers and Newspapers.—Humboldt Courier, New Chronicle.

Physicians.—J. H. Preston, G. W. James, G. W. Penn, Sydney Thompson, R. O. Williams, J. H. Chandler.

Photographers.—J. H. Bailey, Mrs. A. Kernodle.

Produce.—All grocers, E. L. Fox.

Saloons.—J. M. Worthan, C. Peterson, Shane & Boyle, Ed. McHugh, Joe Blakemore.

Tinners.—C. W. Albright.

Undertakers.—Humboldt Mercantile Company, Graham & Johnson.

Postmaster.—C. G. Parker.

Manufactories.—B. C. Jarrell & Co., box factory; Dodson Plow Company, plow factory; Humboldt Marble Works; Eclipse Marble Works; Humboldt Spoke Factory; Humboldt Cotton Mills; Humboldt Hoop and Heading Factory; Humboldt Stave Factory; T. Harden & Co., stave factory; E. W. Ing, flouring mill; Humboldt Ice Factory and Bottling Works.

PLAYHOUSE—CHILDREN OF B. F. JARRELL.

DRUG ESTABLISHMENT OF A. THWEATT, HUMBOLDT

(With Portrait and Sketch of the Doctor).

Dr. A. Thweatt was born in Memphis, Tenn., on September 7, 1870. After the death of his father from yellow fever during the epidemic of 1878, the family moved to

DR. A. THWEATT.

Petersburg, Va., where his mother died in 1879. He came to Humboldt, Tenn., in 1883, where he attended school and was engaged in business with his uncle for about ten years.

He has been engaged in the drug business since 1893. In a competitive examination on pharmacy in New York City in 1899, in which there were 550 contestants, he was awarded a special prize on operative pharmacy. He has been a constant student of the science of his profession (pharmaceutical), and by this means has gained his present high standing in scientific circles. He was appointed by the president of the Tennessee State Druggists' Association, together with Prof. E. A. Ruddiman (Professor of Pharmacy in Vanderbilt University) and Dr. A. Brown Rains, of Columbia, to represent Tennessee in the American Pharmaceutical Association (of which he is a member), which convened at Richmond, Va., in May, 1900.

Although he conducts a general drug store, he pays personal attention to the preparation of medicines and the accurate and scientific compounding of physicians' prescriptions.

Dr. Thweatt's reputation as a conscientious, scientific pharmacist extends over the entire State, and it is a noted fact among his fellow-pharmacists that his drug store is one of the most completely-equipped drug stores in Tennessee. From the following illustrations some idea may be gained of its completeness.

Prescription Department of Dr. Thweatt's Drug Store—His Original Design and Arrangement.

The real character of any drug store can best be judged by inspection of its prescription department. It is the chief department of any good drug store. All else is in a measure subordinate to it.

No expense has been spared in this department to perfect it. Among its excellent fea-

PARTIAL VIEW OF INTERIOR OF DRUG STORE.

tures is a pair of accurate balances which are sensitive to 1-100 of a grain. These balances are fitted with a spirit level and leveling feet, so that they can easily be leveled when necessary. They are also fitted with Russian ag-

PRESCRIPTION DEPARTMENT.

ate bearings. These bearings are not affected by heat or moisture, and hence they do not rust or expand and become inaccurate. This pair of balances is used exclusively for the accurate weighing of potent drugs and chemicals in quantities not heavier than two grains in preparing physicians' prescriptions. There is also a pair of scales in this department which are sensitive to 1-60 of a grain. These are used for the weighing of all substances which enter into prescriptions in quantities of from three grains to one ounce.

The library is also an important feature here. Every necessary book of information on medicine and chemistry is at hand, which adds greatly to the accuracy and convenience of this department. The more potent medicines of this department are kept in a special closet under lock. By this means, when such medicines are wanted, the fact that the door has to be opened before the medicine can be obtained is an additional safeguard against error.

This department is also equipped with a set of special prescription-case shelf ware. The bottles and jars that contain medicines which are affected by light and air are made in amber color to prevent the access of the actinic ray of light (which is the detrimental property), and have ground-glass stoppers, which make them air tight. The more potent medicines which are not affected by light are stored in blue containers of this character, so that they are more easily distinguished from ordinary substances; and the less important medicines are stored in crystal containers of this character, so that their physical identity is readily noted. All of these containers bear labels which are made into the glass, and have the surface of the letters ground opaque. By this means no labels are ever washed or broken off.

This prescription department is finished in white enamel, which provides ample light (a very important feature), and is easily washed and kept clean.

The entire department is inclosed by a wire screen, which renders it impossible for medicines to be handled or the dispenser to be interrupted by outsiders.

A Corner of Laboratory of Thweatt's Drug Store.

In this department important medicinal preparations are prepared personally by Dr. Thweatt, and all drugs and chemicals that are received are examined and tested here before they are placed in stock. If a preparation or

A CORNER OF LABORATORY.

drug does not conform to the standard, it is rejected.

Various chemical tests are also conducted in this department, such as the chemical analysis of urine, etc.

GIBSON COUNTY OF TO-DAY (Continued).

Gibson Wells.

Gibson County has a health resort known throughout West Tennessee for the efficiency of its waters in the cure of some forms of disease. These wells are situated in the southwestern portion of the county, about twelve miles from Trenton, and the same distance from Humboldt. They are reached from either place by carriages furnished by the liverymen. Ample hotel accommodations are provided for visitors, and during the season a great many people from a distance as well as from the near-by cities visit this watering place either for health or amusement. The season lasts from July till October.

There are two establishments for the entertainment and treatment of visitors—one operated by the owners of Gibson Wells proper and the other by the owner and proprietor of what is designated as New Gibson Wells. The latter is operated by Mr. J. F. Watt, whose hotel and cottages for permanent visitors occupy ground adjacent to the Old Gibson Wells property.

The water of New Gibson Wells is thought by some to be superior to that of the Old. At any rate, the medicinal virtue of the water furnished by Mr. Watt's wells has been tested in the cure of stomach, bowel, and kidney complaints in numerous cases, and has proved equal to any in the country. Many invalids have gone away from these springs entirely cured of their maladies. Mr. Watt is an obliging landlord, and takes pains to secure the comfort and proper entertainment of his guests.

Speaking of the farming interests in this section of the county, I found the lands in the Fourth, Fifth, and Twentieth Districts generally good and the farmers, as a class, industrious, prosperous, and progressive.

About Gibson Wells, Fruitland, and Brazil are some extensive farms. Bailey & Son have large farming interests. I had the pleasure of being entertained at the homes of some of these people while passing through, and found them hospitable, courteous, and well posted in general information, and universally moral and religious.

I want to mention Mr. Joe H. McClaran, at whose home I visited, as a remarkable farmer, who will answer as a type of all. Mr. McClaran has a small farm—perhaps 150 acres—but everything about his farm shows intelligent and scientific supervision. His method aims at the best in every particular. His dwelling and its convenience, his barns and provisions for the care of stock, the treatment and care of his land, the culture of his crops—all show him to be a model farmer. He operates a cotton gin and a steam thresher, and is a busy, prosperous man, and a good one.

Transportation Facilities.

The prosperity and importance of Gibson County is due largely to the system of railroads that traverse its territory. There are three important railroads passing through the county, furnishing complete access to outside markets, as well as local intercommunication.

The Mobile and Ohio Railroad is the oldest railroad in the county. This railroad was built in 1856 and 1857, and passes through the county from north to south, establishing direct communication with Northern and Southern markets. This road furnishes most excellent and reliable service, both as to freight and passenger traffic, and the roadbed and rolling stock are maintained in fine condition. Trenton, Humboldt, Dyer, Rutherford, Kenton, Fruitland—all large shipping and trading points—are on its line.

The Louisville and Nashville Railroad traverses the county from near the middle of the eastern border to the southwest corner, having about seventeen miles of its line in the county. This great railroad, furnishing an outlet to the great markets of the North and East and to the great cotton market of Memphis, has been, and is to-day, a powerful factor in creating and maintaining the commercial and manufacturing interests of the county and supporting and promoting agricultural development. The cities of Humboldt and Milan are on this road, as also the thriving village and shipping point of Gibson Station.

GIBSON COUNTY, TENNESSEE. ILLUSTRATED. 79

The Illinois Central Railroad passes from north to south through the eastern side of the county, giving to the people of that section a choice of routes to the Northern and Southern markets. The city of Milan is on this road, as also the prosperous villages of Medina and Bradford, both important shipping points. Other stations on this road are Idlewild and Cades.

It can readily be seen that a county possessing the natural endowments that Gibson has, and with such facilities for transportation, must needs take a front rank among the counties of the State.

The Masonic Fraternity in Gibson County.

This noble order has a strong membership in the county and is increasing in numbers and influence. There are in the State of Tennessee 427 Master Masons' lodges, with 17,343 members, as shown by last Grand Lodge report.

SOME OF THE DRUMMERS OF GIBSON COUNTY.

1, H. N. Tharp, Humboldt, with Rankin-Snyder Hardware Company, Louisville, Ky.; 2, L. F. McWherter, Trenton, with Bayless Bros. & Co., queensware, Louisville, Ky.; 3, George French, Trenton, with W. C. Early & Co., Memphis, Tenn.; 4, P. T. Yarbrough, Trenton, with American Snuff Company, New York; 5, G. S. Lannom, Humboldt, with Ferguson-McKinney Dry Goods Company, St. Louis; 6, W. B. Mills, Trenton, with W. B. Belknap Company, hardware, Louisville, Ky.; 7, A. N. Gordon, Dyer, with Frank G. Fite, pianos and organs, Nashville, Tenn.; 8, J. H. Holmes, Dyer, with Dyer Fruit Box Manufacturing Company, Dyer, Tenn.; 9, W. F. Stewart, Milan, with the Tilden Company, chemists, New York and St. Louis; 10, Andrew J. Johnson, Trenton, with the McCormick Company, Chicago, Ill.; 11, W. S. Shocklett, Fulton, hardware.

In Gibson County there is a total membership of 343 in the master's degree, divided among the following lodges:

The oldest lodge in the county is Trenton Lodge No. 86, organized in 1838. This lodge has now a membership of 41. T. J. Happel is Worshipful Master and T. Harlan is Secretary. It meets on the second Monday in each month.

Yorkville Lodge No. 115, at Yorkville, has 36 members and holds its meetings on Thursday before the full moon in each month, at 2 P.M. J. C. Carlton is Worshipful Master and J. T. Carlton is Secretary.

Milan Lodge No. 191, at Milan, has a membership of 20, and meets on Saturday before the fourth Sunday in each month. W. H. Alger is Worshipful Master and T. L. Harmon is Secretary.

Humboldt Lodge No. 202, at Humboldt, has 48 members, and meets on the second Friday night in each month. N. A. Senter is Worshipful Master and John M. Senter is Secretary.

Eaton Lodge No. 206, at Eaton, has 21 members, and meets Wednesday on or before full moon. G. E. Carlton is Worshipful Master and J. W. Smith is Secretary.

Bone Lodge No. 252, at Rutherford, has 51 members, and meets on the second Monday in each month. J. W. C. Fain is Worshipful Master and W. P. McCallum is Secretary.

Dyer Lodge No. 357, at Dyer, has 37 members, and meets every first Thursday in the month at 2 P.M. W. B. Halliburton is Worshipful Master and R. R. Kenton is Secretary.

Medina Lodge No. 399, at Medina, has 32 members, and meets every fourth Saturday at 1:30 P.M. J. E. Adkisson is Worshipful Master and B. A. Taylor is Secretary.

Rolla Lodge No. 465, at Bradford, has 54 members, and meets every Saturday before the second Sunday in the month. Milton Brown is Worshipful Master and J. N. Rochelle is Secretary.

W. H. Dodd.

William Henry, son of J. M. and P. P. Dodd, was born in the Sixth District of Gibson County, Tenn., on March 16, 1851. The Civil War coming on when he was only ten years old and the responsibility of the farm falling on him as the oldest son, he did not enjoy the advantages of an early school

W. H. DODD.

education. Like thousands of other sons of our Southern heroes, he had to give all his time to the support of the family, while the father did service upon the battlefield; but along the educational line a sufficient height has been attained, by close individual study, to make life a reasonable success and to accomplish all that an ambitious mind has led him to undertake.

On May 17, 1877, he was married to Mrs. Lucy Strong, daughter of Capt. T. W. Williams; and to them have been born four children—Elmon, Allen, Robert, and Annie. Three of these are now living, Allen having died on October 7, 1899.

When married, Mr. Dodd settled on a farm near Brazil, in the Fifth District of this county, where he resided until 1899, when he moved with his family to Trenton for the purpose of giving the children better educational advantages.

While on the farm, he devoted his time to stock raising especially and farming in general, and in these pursuits was reasonably successful.

In the year 1892 he engaged in the manufacture of lumber with Mr. W. T. Ingram, under the firm name of Ingram & Dodd. The success of this business was encouraging enough to induce him to purchase Mr. Ingram's interest in the mills, which he did in 1898. He is still operating the same near Brazil.

Having a natural love for mathematics, he, in 1897, became deeply interested in the science of surveying, and at once obtained instruments and books for the study of the same. By individual efforts he acquired a proficiency in this art, and was solicited to accept a deputyship under County Surveyor L. W. Morgan. He did so, and met with much encouragement in this work. At the January (1901) term of the County Court he was elected for a four-years' term of office as County Surveyor, the duties of which he is now discharging.

Mr. Dodd is a most exemplary and upright citizen, esteemed for his noble qualities of heart and mind by his intimate friends, and popular with the general public for his obliging disposition and strict devotion to his public duties.

Taxables of County by Districts.

(Tables showing number of acres of land and number of town lots, with valuation; also value of personal property and number of polls, compiled from assessor's books of 1900.)

Total number of acres assessed for taxation, 355,816; total value, $3,337,725.

Total value of town lots, $1,351,600.

Total personal property given in for taxation, $529,090.

Total number of polls, 5,566.

Total taxables, $5,218,415.

Average assessed value of land per acre, $9.38.

Total levy, State and county, $1.35.

District No. 1:
Acres 14,280
Value $126,378
Lots 47
Value 18,375
Personals 4,000

Total taxables $148,753

District No. 2:
Acres 14,434
Value $130,275
Personals 5,400

Total $135,675

District No. 3 (Humboldt):
Acres 18,657
Value $184,900
Lots 647
Value 367,825
Personals 138,100

Total $690,825

District No. 4 (Gibson Wells):
Acres 7,448
Value 59,325
Lots 3
Value 550
Personals 2,025

Total $61,900

District No. 5 (Brazil):
Acres 13,935
Value $128,000
Lots 21
Value 3,350
Personals 3,325

Total $134,675

District No. 6:
Acres 22,010
Value $148,700
Lots 29
Value 2,700
Personals 2,475

Total $153,875

District No. 7 (Trenton):
Acres 22,815
Value $251,550
Lots 485
Value 454,800
Personals 201,515

Total $907,865

District No. 8 (Yorkville):

Acres	23,401	
Value		$253,650
Lots	33	
Value		12,750
Personals		8,725
Total		$275,125

District No. 9 (Rutherford):

Acres	11,448	
Value		$127,650
Lots	140	
Value		79,800
Personals		35,625
Total		$243,075

District No. 10 (Kenton):

Acres	13,056	
Value		$148,000
Lots	70	
Value		27,025
Personals		4,150
Total		$179,175

District No. 11:

Acres	14,675	
Value		$151,950
Personals		4,875
Total		$156,825

District No. 12:

Acres	15,720	
Value		$111,600
Personals		2,300
Total		$113,900

District No. 13 (Milan):

Acres	26,433	
Value		$265,900
Lots	420	
Value		262,275
Personals		47,900
Total		$576,075

District No. 14 (Bradford):

Acres	15,666	
Value		$128,250
Lots	63	
Value		19,150
Personals		36,800
Total		$184,200

District No. 15:

Acres	14,489	
Value		$83,200
Personals		5,625
Total		$88,825

District No. 16:

Acres	13,002	
Value		$115,400
Personals		1,875
Total		$117,275

District No. 17:

Acres	10,823	
Value		$62,800
Personals		3,050
Total		$65,850

District No. 18 (Gibson):

Acres	13,111	
Value		$139,800
Lots	11	
Value		3,150
Personals		2,175
Total		$145,125

District No. 19:

Acres	16,259	
Value		$145,125
Personals		1,425
Total		$146,550

District No 20 (Fruitland):

Acres	5,906	
Value		$64,200
Lots	7	
Value		1,850
Total		$66,050

District No. 21 (Dyer):

Acres	15,204	
Value		$193,050
Lots	190	
Value		97,925
Personals		10,525
Total		$301,500

District No. 22:

Acres	7,997	
Value		$ 52,000
Lots	3	
Value		75
Personals		250
Total		$ 52,325

District No. 23:

Acres	10,026	
Value		$ 80,850
Personals		800
Total		$ 81,650

District No. 24:

Acres	11,969	
Value		$154,200
Personals		6,050
Total		$160,250

District No. 25:

Acres	2,989	
Value		$ 30,975
Personals		100
Total		$ 31,075

The county is out of debt, except $20,000 of interest-bearing warrants, issued for the completion of the courthouse. About one-half the cost of the courthouse has already been paid in cash.

Warrants for the ordinary expenses of the county are paid in cash by the county trustee on demand.

GRANDFATHER COLLINSWORTH
(A pioneer of Gibson County, father of A. J. Collinsworth).

OLD ANCESTRAL HOME OF A. J. COLLINSWORTH, NEAR HUMBOLDT.

CITY OF TRENTON.

EARLY HISTORY.

The city of Trenton is the capital town of the county of Gibson, and is situated near the center of the county on what was formerly the Mobile and Ohio Railroad, now a part of the Southern Railway. It is 232 miles from St. Louis, 474 miles from New Orleans, 306 miles from Louisville, 92 miles from Memphis, 185 miles from Nashville, and 440 miles from Chicago. It is the oldest town in the county, having been settled before the county was organized. Before it became the county seat it was called "Gibsonport," after Thomas F. Gibson, who had made a settlement and engaged in general merchandising there about 1821.

When the county was organized in 1823, commissioners were appointed by the legislature to select a site for the county seat of the new county. They fixed upon the spot occupied by Thomas F. Gibson. The record reads that "the county seat was located upon twenty acres of land on which the town of Gibsonport is in part situated, part of a 1,700-acre tract, entered by John B. Hogg and John Whitaker." The commissioners obtained from Hogg and Whitaker and others (see history of county) donations of land for the county seat amounting to fifty-six and a quarter acres, which constituted the original site of Trenton. This land was laid off into lots, alleys, and streets, and sold by commissioners appointed by the County Court.

The commissioners who laid off the town and sold the lots were: John H. Rains, John P. Thomas, John Parker, Robert Tinkle, and John W. Evans. The plan of the town of Trenton delineating the public square and locating the lots and streets upon the first twenty acres donated by Hogg and Whitaker, was entered on record at the March (1829) term of the Court of Pleas and Quarter Sessions. This is the only plan of the town on file in the records of the county. The lots laid off on the original fifty acres were soon disposed of, and additions were made to the town by parties owning lands adjacent. In 1847, when the town was first incorporated, the lines of incorporation embraced about 144 acres.

The growth of Trenton as a town kept pace with the settlement and development of the county. It was not a phenomenal growth, but a steady and substantial advance.

From the time of the location of the county seat at Trenton up to the period when the Mobile and Ohio and the Louisville and Nashville Railroads were built through the county, Trenton was the principal center of trade and influence in the county. There were but few other towns in the county, and the county being sparsely settled in those early times, most of the trading and marketing of the people was done at the county seat.

The population of Trenton in 1834 was about 400. In 1860 it was 1,200. During the Civil War the town suffered in common with all other towns of the South and did not recover its former importance for several years after the close of the war.

In 1870 the population was about 1,000. The establishment of the Trenton Cotton Mills, the Trenton Cottonseed Oil Mill, the stave and saw mills, and the flouring mill industries added largely to the population and commercial importance of the town, so that in 1890 the population had grown to nearly 2,000.

The United States census, just completed, gives the population of Trenton in 1900 as 2,328. This only includes persons living within the corporate limits. The town, including the outlying suburbs, contains a population of nearly 3,000 souls.

The Trenton of to-day is a prosperous and

busy little city, whose people are imbued with a spirit of progress that will not allow their city to lag behind in the march of improvement.

The city has a splendid system of water works, the property of the corporation, and is lighted by electricity.

It has four handsome brick churches and a well-conducted graded school, whose curriculum embraces the higher branches of an English education, as well as the introductory branches of a classical education.

The streets of the town are well laid off and fringed with shade trees of box elder, elm, and maple, presenting a pleasing aspect of sylvan beauty. Upon the principal residence streets and in the environs of the town are many beautiful residences, testifying to the taste and prosperity of the people.

The social structure of Trenton is the growth of years. It has the element of maturity imparted by time and the survival of the best in human character. Being for a long time the center of business and influence in the county and always the seat of the county government, it attracted those bent upon a career in the professions, in politics, and in business. It became, therefore, and still is, the principal seat of learning, education, and culture in the county.

OAK MANOR, RESIDENCE OF W. L. SMITH, TRENTON.

MUNICIPALITY OF TRENTON.

The Act incorporating the town of Trenton was passed on December 14, 1847. The town government was styled "the Mayor and Aldermen of the town of Trenton." It consisted of a Mayor and six Aldermen, Town Constable, and Recorder, holding office for twelve months. The powers and duties of these officers were defined in a general provision, providing that they should be such as were conferred by the charter of the town of Jackson on the officers of that town. The boundaries of the corporation were as follows: Beginning at the northwest corner of the town as designated by the original plan of the town, which is registered in the Register's office of Gibson County, in Book B, page 89; running thence east 114 poles to a stake; thence south 202 poles to a stake; thence west 114 poles to a stake; thence north 202 poles to beginning; said corporation to have control of six and one-half acres adjoining said town on the north, conveyed to said town for a common, and also the graveyard belonging to the town, with power to inclose or otherwise improve the same. Act of March 9, 1867, amended above so as to include the territory lying west and south of said corporation, bounded as follows: Beginning at the northwest corner of said corporation, running due west to the Mobile and Ohio Railroad; thence south with said road to a point south, opposite an alley along the south boundary, to include the lots of McGee, Richardson, Davis, Pearce, Caldwell, and others, to a point opposite southeast corner of said corporation; and thence north to connect with the southeast corner of said corporation. This Act was amended on March 31, 1881, and all Acts pertaining to the municipality of Trenton were considered. The Act was again amended on March 27,

1892, and on May 10, 1895, further enlarging the powers of the corporation. In March, 1890, power was conferred upon the municipality to issue waterworks bonds.

At present the municipal government of the city of Trenton consists of the following-named officers:

L. H. Tyree is Mayor.

The city is divided into three wards, each having two members in the City Council. The members of the Council in the first ward are J. Freed and R. C. Ward; in the second ward, E. E. Benton and R. H. Moore; and in the third ward, T. J. Happel and M. W. Lain.

The City Treasurer is T. J. Happel; and the Recorder, who has the powers of a magistrate, is Jesse R. Smith.

W. W. Ezell is City Marshall, with the powers of a constable; and R. O. Green is night policeman.

The Mayor and members of the legislative council are elected by the qualified voters of the city for one year. The other officers are appointed by the Mayor and Council.

The waterworks, which are now owned by the city, were constructed by private parties in 1897 and were bought by the city two years later. The parties who built and owned the plant were: Charles Regan, R. H. Wade, John R. Walker, G. R. Howse, and others. The plant cost the city $14,500, for which it issued bonds running twenty years and bearing six per cent interest, payable at the option of the city. A number of the bonds have been paid off, and the entire debt will be extinguished long before the twenty years expire. The waterworks are managed by a board, consisting of T. J. Happel, City Treasurer, who is chairman, and E. E. Benton and J. Freed.

The electric light plant of the city is owned by private parties, W. P. Keenan and C. L. Wade. The plant is deficient in equipment for the needs of a city like Trenton, and is not patronized to the extent it would be if more efficient. The public lights are not of sufficient candle power nor of sufficient number, and the lighting of the churches, stores, and private residences is unsatisfactory. The plant is only operated half the night. It would be better if the city owned the plant and put in an equipment that would meet the wants of the city.

The Fire Department of the city is managed by a fire marshal, who is at the head of

FACULTY OF PEABODY HIGH SCHOOL, TRENTON.

an organized company, who are paid when called in service. The resources for the extinguishment of fires consists of two hose carts carrying 900 feet of two-inch hose, and a hook and ladder wagon fully equipped.

Peabody High School is the name given to the public school of Trenton. The Board of Education consists of the school directors of the district. These directors are at present T. E. Harwood, C. W. Patton, and R. B. Wade. There are eleven grades taught in this school, three more grades than provided in the State curriculum. The school is maintained by the general school fund, supplemented by a donation from the city of Trenton of five hundred dollars per annum. The school is free to the children of the district in all the grades up to and including the eighth. Tuition in the three high-school grades is charged for. The faculty of the school is composed of able and experienced teachers, selected for their ability as teachers. The following constitute the faculty of the institution:

F. L. Dennison, principal.
—— Davis, first assistant.
Miss Emma Owen, second assistant.
Miss Latta Biggs, third assistant.
Mrs. Florence Green, fourth assistant.
Miss Mai McRee, fifth assistant.
Miss Mettie D. Pearce, sixth assistant.
Miss Lessie Keenan, seventh assistant.
Mrs. Mattie Fielder, eighth assistant.
Miss Mattie Butler, ninth assistant.

BEN. OPPENHEIMER
(Leading photographer of Trenton).

CHURCHES OF TRENTON.

The Baptist Church of Trenton.

This church was organized on August 23, 1850, with a membership of twenty-five persons. From the time of its organization down to the present time it has not only grown and

REV. J. H. BUTLER
(Pastor Baptist Church, Trenton).

prospered in itself, but has been, in a sense, the parent of four other church organizations. Hickory Grove, Beech Grove, Trenton (colored), and Center Churches all owe, in a degree, their organization to the mother church of Trenton.

Trenton Church has had as pastors in its history some of the ablest ministers in the Baptist denomination. Rev. Mathew Hilman, one of the ablest and most zealous Baptist ministers in Tennessee, was pastor of the church for twenty-one years. W. H. Ryals, another distinguished Baptist minister, was its pastor for fifteen years.

Some of the deacons of the church have served for a still longer period. In this capacity J. M. Senter has served forty years and still officiates; L. M. Jones, twenty-seven years; J. C. McDearmon, twenty-two years; R. N. Davis, twenty-two years; and J. A. McDearmon, twenty-one years.

The present beautiful house of worship was built in 1885, and is a splendid monument to the taste, liberality, and zeal of the membership. The present membership of the church is 214. Rev. J. H. Butler assumed the pastorate of the church in 1900.

The Sunday school of the church was organized in April, 1866, and now numbers 165 on its roll. A remarkable fact in the history of this Sunday school is that during its existence of thirty-six years it has had but three superintendents, one of whom, J. M. Senter, served for thirty-four years of the time; J. A. McDearmon and R. R. Caldwell serving one year each. After serving thirty-four years, Mr. Senter resigned last year, on account of

BAPTIST CHURCH, TRENTON.

failing health, and was succeeded by W. H. Haste, who is the present superintendent.

The prayer meeting of the church every Wednesday night dates from 1871.

The church maintains a Ladies' Missionary Society, Ladies' Aid Society, and Young Ladies' Aid Society, all of which are flourishing and efficient in their several fields of work.

The Methodist Episcopal Church of Trenton.

The Methodist Church in Trenton is probably the oldest church organization in the city. An effort was made to organize a church here as early as 1826, but it was not altogether successful. However, a society was formed and trustees appointed to secure the means to build a church; but the house was not completed till 1834. A station was established in 1839 and Benj. H. Hubbard was its first pastor. In 1844 Trenton Station was abolished, at the request of the members, and resumed its place in the Trenton Circuit, with J. W. McFarland as circuit rider.

In 1846 the church at Trenton again became a station, and has so remained ever since. Its first pastor after becoming a station in 1846 was B. A. Hays. Since then the church has steadily grown and prospered, both in membership and influence, and now has the largest membership of any church in the city. It has a beautiful and capacious church building, erected at a cost of fourteen thousand dollars, and a total membership of over three hundred.

The pastor of the church for the present year is Rev. S. L. Jewell. The officers are: Stewards—R. C. Adams, chairman; H. M. Elder, treasurer; A. W. Biggs, secretary; R. W. Harrison, Doak Harrison, J. H. Hefley, B. F. Jones, Quintin Rankin; J. T. Warren, recording steward. Trustees—J. W. Elder, John Hassell, Dr. Z. Biggs, T. J. Happel, H. M. Elder, E. E. Benton, J. R. Deason, B. F. Jones, and Sp'l Hill.

REV. S. L. JEWELL
(Pastor Methodist Episcopal Church of Trenton).

TRENTON METHODIST CHURCH.

The Sunday school has 185 pupils enrolled. This is the oldest Sunday school in the county. It was organized in 1850. John W. Elder

REV. W. J. NAYLOR
(Pastor Trenton Circuit, Methodist Episcopal Church).

was elected its first superintendent and served continuously for forty-nine years and until incapacitated by ill health. The present superintendent is J. T. Warren, who succeeded Mr. Elder in 1899.

The Presbyterian Church.

The Presbyterian Church in Trenton was organized in 1833, Messrs. Moses Woodfin, J. M. Carthel, and Dr. J. H. Crisp being the first elders. Other elders of the church before the war were Messrs. Ben. Elder, A. A. P. Grigsby, J. D. McDowell, John I. McCulloch, Judge Black, and T. J. Carthel.

In 1845 they built their first house of worship, on High street, near the central part of the town. The building is still standing opposite the Hotel Bigelow. Their pastors before the war were Rev. Messrs. Sloan, Moses Hodge, A. T. Graves, and Dr. Bright. Dr. Campbell and Dr. Anderson supplied the pulpit during the war. Dr. J. H. McNeilly, now of Nashville, was called to the pastorate after the war, and was succeeded by Dr. M. M. Marshall, who continued with the church for a number of years. Rev. P. D. Stephenson

REV. T. M. HUNTER
(Pastor Presbyterian Church).

followed Dr. Marshall and was succeeded by Rev. J. T. Rothrock, who was pastor for fourteen years. Rev. Wallace T. Palmer, now of New Orleans, was pastor for two years and was succeeded by the present pastor, Rev. T.

M. Hunter, who came to this church in October, 1897.

In 1892 the church secured the present convenient site, on the corner of High and Fourth streets, and built the beautiful church in which they now worship. It was dedicated in 1893, and is considered one of the handsomest and most convenient church edifices in West Tennessee.

The present officers of the church are: Elders—Judge J. T. Carthel, Judge M. M. Neil, R. E. Grizzard, W. W. Wade, E. A. Herron, and W. A. Skiles. Deacons—J. E. Carthel, H. H. Wade, N. L. McRee, W. L. Wade, W. W. Lain, C. F. Givens, L. E. Carne, and Hal Partee.

On June 29, 1899, the church dismissed one of its elders, Mr. W. F. McRee, and about twenty members, to organize a church near McRee's Schoolhouse.

PRESBYTERIAN CHURCH OF TRENTON.

This colony of the church is in a growing and flourishing condition. Other missions are sustained by this church, which is thoroughly alive in all evangelistic and philanthropic enterprises.

Cumberland Presbyterian Church of Trenton.

The church at Trenton was organized in 1848. The members constituting the church at its first organization were: O. B. Caldwell, M. B. King, John A. Wilkins, Samuel Zaricor, John Kimbrough, Benjamin A. Bailey, M. M. Houston, Smith Parkes, and Nelson I. Hess. The ruling elders were: M. M. Houston, Samuel Zaricor, Smith Parkes, John Kimbrough, and M. B. King; J. A. Wilkins, deacon; Smith Parkes, clerk.

The following were some of the early pastors of Trenton Church: N. I. Hess, C. I. Bradley, Mr. Hubert, H. B. Warren,

CUMBERLAND PRESBYTERIAN CHURCH, TRENTON.

SOME PORTRAITS, PICTURES, AND SKETCHES IN AND ABOUT TRENTON.

Gibson County Bank, Trenton.

This is the oldest banking institution in Gibson County. The history of banking in Gibson County is briefly told. From the creation of the county in 1823 up to 1838 the people were without banking facilities. In the latter year a branch of the State Bank of Tennessee was located at Trenton, with Moses Woodfin as president and John A. Taliaferro as cashier. The affairs of this branch bank were managed by a board of directors, composed of citizens of the county, appointed by the officers of the State Bank. These directors were often changed during the twenty-two years of the bank's operations in the county. Some of those remembered were: Col. Edwin Sharp, Joseph W. Carthel, Benjamin Elder, John L. Davis, Thomas J. Freeman, afterwards one of the supreme judges of the State; and John W. Elder, now president of the Gibson County Bank.

Immediately after the commencement of the war between the States, the funds of the bank were removed South and the bank was not again reopened. For a long period after the war closed, the business interests of the county were unrepresented by any banking institution.

In 1879 the Gibson County Bank was organized under special charter of the Legislature of Tennessee, with an authorized capital of $25,000. Shortly afterwards the capital was increased to $50,000.

The bank was organized with John W. Elder as president and H. M. Elder as cashier. These officers have continued at the head of the institution ever since.

In 1883 A. S. Elder, a grandson of President Elder, was made assistant cashier; and in 1897 Thomas K. Happel, another grandson of President Elder, was made bookkeeper. This constitutes the present administrative force of the institution.

The Gibson County Bank has enjoyed a prosperous career since its first establishment, proving a strong factor in the development and support of the business interests of the people. Its affairs have been ably and conservatively managed, and it stands today as one among the solid financial institutions of West Tennessee. It has recently declared its forty-second dividend, and its history shows that it has paid a dividend of five per cent upon its stock semiannually since its organization.

GIBSON COUNTY BANK.

John W. Elder.

There are but few men now living in the city of Trenton whose lives are more intimately connected with the commercial and social history of the place than that of John W. Elder, whose portrait appears on next page. Mr. Elder has been identified with the growth and development of the town of Trenton almost from the period of its birth.

The town was located in 1824 and Mr. Elder became one of its citizens in 1835. From that time forward for more than sixty-seven years, except about three years spent in Alabama during and after the Civil War, he has been a prominent and active figure in the affairs of the town and county.

Mr. Elder is well known to the business world as merchant and banker, his long career in these pursuits having given him an extensive acquaintance throughout the country. He is the oldest merchant and banker in the county, and, with few exceptions, the oldest citizen.

JOHN W. ELDER
(President Gibson County Bank).

Mr. Elder came to Trenton from Rutherford County, Tenn., when a lad of fifteen, in the year 1835. At that time Trenton was but a small village, but it was the county seat and the center of a growing trade.

After serving several years as a merchant's clerk, thus acquiring a knowledge of the mercantile business, he began business for himself, continuing the same until the breaking out of the Civil War, in 1861. During this period he was connected with the management of the branch of the State Bank of Tennessee at Trenton as one of the directors, 1850-1854.

At the close of the Civil War, finding conditions unfavorable for business at his home on account of the unsettled state of the country during the so-called reconstruction period, Mr. Elder became a member of the mercantile firm of Duncan, Ford & Elder, of Cincinnati, Ohio, traveling for his firm in the South, but still making his home at Trenton. He continued with this firm until 1878, when he closed out his interest; and in June, 1879, together with H. M. Elder and others, he organized the Gibson County Bank, of which he is now president.

In 1885 Mr. Elder, with others, organized the Trenton Cotton Mill Company, an industry that has been most beneficial to the county and whose product is well known in the markets of the country.

While Mr. Elder has been a conspicuous figure in the business and civil affairs of Trenton, perhaps the best and most useful side of his life has been that which distinguished him as an active paticipant and oftentimes a leader in the religious and educational movements of the people. Certainly, his life in this regard may well be taken as a model by our young men starting upon a business career.

At the early age of fourteen he professed religion and joined the Methodist Church, and in 1835 became a member of the church at Trenton, retaining his membership therein ever since.

In 1850 he was elected superintendent of the Sunday school of the Methodist Church at Trenton, which position he held for forty-nine consecutive years. In the spring of 1899, owing to a severe attack of la grippe, he was compelled to resign, after having served his people for a longer consecutive period, perhaps, than any other officer in Sunday school annals. He has continuously served as an officer in the local church organization in some helpful capacity, and is at present one of the trustees of the church. He is now, and has been since its creation, treasurer of the Board of Church Extension of the Memphis Conference of the Methodist Episcopal Church.

Mr. Elder married Miss Martha G. Huston, of Alabama, in 1841, a noble Christian lady, who remained by his side, contributing to his success and sharing in his disappointments until July 23, 1879, when she was called away.

Mr. Elder has six living children, all occupying honorable positions in the social and business world. Since the death of his wife Mr. Elder has remained single, spending the remaining years of a useful and honorable life quietly and serenely in the society of his children and grandchildren and among the people endeared to him by long association.

He is still strong and vigorous in mind and body, performing the duties of president of the Gibson County Bank with the same promptitude and dispatch that distinguished his earlier years.

occupied as boiler and engine and batt, picker, and spool rooms. The lower story of the factory building is used as a weaving room, where are operated 160 looms. The second story is used for spinning and carding. Here are operated 6,000 spindles and forty cards.

The entire industry gives employment to one hundred and sixty operatives, with a weekly pay roll of $600. The motive power of the mills is furnished by a Hamilton Corless engine of two hundred horse power, and three boilers with a combined production of two hundred and eighty horse power. The fire protection provided is ample, consisting of the latest improved au-

TRENTON COTTON MILLS.

Trenton Cotton Mills.

One of the most extensive and useful industries in Gibson County is the Trenton Cotton Mills, located in the city of Trenton.

The Trenton Cotton Mill Company was organized in 1884 and incorporated by special act of the Legislature in that year. The buildings constituting the plant are all of brick, except the ginnery, which is a detached frame standing some distance from the main factory, constituting a separate department, though only operated in ginning cotton for use in the mill.

The main factory building is 50x365 feet, two stories high, with two one-story wings

tomatic sprinklers and hose connections with the city water mains. The plant is lighted by its own electric light system, using over two hundred incandescent lights, of thirty-two candle power each.

Two thousand bales of raw ginned cotton are converted into cloth and battings per annum, about eighteen hundred bales into sheetings and drills, and two hundred into batting. The output of the mill in woven goods is upwards of 250,000 yards per annum. The entire stock of cotton used by the Trenton Cotton Mills is bought from local producers, thus giving a home market to the cotton raisers of the county.

The brands of sheetings manufactured and well known in the markets are its AAA 4-4 and BB 7-8 sheetings, and its AAA 12, 14, and 16-oz. drills. A special quality of drilling is made for pockets for pants manufacturers.

The product of the Trenton Cotton Mills is marketed in the States of the South and Southwest and in the Middle States, and has always found a ready market.

The officers of the Trenton Cotton Mills are: J. A. Landis, president; George W. Everett, secretary, treasurer, and general manager. The directors are John W. Elder, T. J. Happel, T. J. Hays, G. W. Everett, and J. A. Landis.

Meyer Oppenheimer.

Here is a picture of an old and eminent citizen of Trenton, now dead, but whose memory is revered by all who knew him in life and by many who have been benefited by his foresight in promoting the welfare of the town and community.

Meyer Oppenheimer became a citizen of Trenton sometime in the fifties, coming here from Hickman, Ky., where he had been in business. The building of the railroad through Gibson County, noticed in another article, deprived Hickman of a great deal of its trade, and Mr. Oppenheimer removed his business to Trenton. He soon became one of the leading merchants of the place and was noted for his benevolence and the interest he took in the general welfare. His philanthropy was unbounded, and no cry for aid from a fellow mortal ever fell unheeded upon his ear.

Although of foreign birth and an adherent of the Jewish Church, he was thoroughly American in his ideas of government, and his religion was a practical recognition of the brotherhood of the whole human family. I do not think I have been guilty of exaggeration in thus speaking of the character of this noble man. It is the universal verdict of the people of Trenton with whom I have talked.

Mr. Oppenheimer was elected thrice to the Mayoralty of the town and served frequently as a member of the town Board of Aldermen and in other public positions, always exemplifying a singleness of purpose in his devotion to public duty. The beautiful shade trees that adorn many of the streets are the result of his enterprise and persistent effort. His public spirit was manifest in providing sidewalks for the streets and in beautifying and adorning the public cemetery. He was forward in all charitable movements for helping the poor and for alleviating distress wherever found. It is related of him that on one occasion after the war a number of returning Confederate soldiers passed through Trenton on their way home, foot-sore, hungry, and al-

MEYER OPPENHEIMER.

most naked. Mr. Oppenheimer set to work to relieve their necessities, and finding no one to assist him in his charitable design, fed and clothed them at his own expense. During the Civil War he was noted for the aid and care he gave to the families of those who were off in the war.

Mr. Oppenheimer was born in Germany on December 17, 1817, and came to America in 1847. He came to Trenton in 1855. After a long and useful life, he died in Chicago, on November 1, 1895. His children who survive him are : Mr. Louis Oppenheimer, of Trenton; Messrs. Henry and Samuel Oppenheimer, of Memphis; Mrs. E. Solomon, of Chicago; and Miss Cora Oppenheimer, of Logansport, Ind.

Exchange Bank of Trenton.

The Exchange Bank of Trenton was organized under the general laws of the State in June, 1887, with a capital of $50,000. The original incorporators of the bank were J. M. Senter, J. T. Carthel, R. A. Hicks, R. Z. Taylor, J. E. Carthel, R. M. Russell, and Henry Flowers, all citizens of Trenton, except Mr. Flowers, who lived at Kenton.

While not as old an institution as the Gibson County Bank, the Exchange Bank has experienced a very profitable career and transacts an extensive business.

The present officers of the bank are: J. M. Senter, president; J. E. Carthel, cashier; J. T. Warren, assistant cashier; and J. D. McKnight, bookkeeper. Mr. Senter and Mr. Carthel have occupied these positions since its organization.

J. M. Senter.

Mr. J. M. Senter, a short sketch of whose life I give below, is one among Gibson County's oldest and most respected citizens. He stands at the head of one of the important financial institutions of the town in which he has made his home for nearly half a century. He has been identified with much of the business and growth of the town and has helped to forward in a marked degree its religious and educational interests. A member of the Baptist Church in Trenton since 1858, he served as the superintendent of its Sunday school for a period of thirty-four years, only relinquishing his charge when failing health rendered him unequal to the duties of the position. His zeal in the promotion of religion and morals, his uprightness as a citizen and man of business, has secured for him the confidence of his fellow-citizens all over the county.

Mr. Senter was born in Cumberland County, N. C., on August 13, 1827. His parents emigrated to Tennessee in 1830, living for short periods in Bedford and Madison Counties, finally settling in Gibson County in 1835. He was brought up on a farm, participating in its life and labors until he was twenty years old. In 1849 he engaged in the mercantile business as a clerk in a country store, near where Humboldt now stands.

In January, 1856, he engaged in the dry goods business for himself at Enterprise, eight and a half miles southeast of Trenton. In July, 1858, he removed to Trenton and engaged in the dry goods business under the firm name of Senter & Wilkins, continuing the same until the breaking out of the Civil War.

J. M. SENTER
(President of Exchange Bank of Trenton).

In June, 1865, he, with Dr. Zach Biggs, opened a hardware and grocery store in Trenton, operating the same for nearly three years, when his health failing he went to farming. He remained on his farm until 1887, when, with others, he organized the Exchange Bank of Trenton, of which he was elected president, retaining that office down to the present time.

I do not think it has been Mr. Senter's ambition through life to become a rich man, though his career shows that he has been an industrious and provident one, securing a competency for old age by the exercise of these virtues. But his name and fame among his fellow-citizens show that he has been a just and helpful man in all his social relations, and this will keep his memory green after life's fitful dream is over.

Harrison Dry Goods Company.

The accompanying cut represents the first floor of this immense establishment. The

INTERIOR VIEW OF THE HARRISON DRY GOODS COMPANY'S STORE, TRENTON.

business was organized on January 1, 1900, and is the largest dry goods, clothing, and shoe house in Gibson County. It pays the largest State and county tax of any business concern in the county. It is composed of Russell W. Harrison, president; S. Horace McKenzie, vice president; Hart H. Wade, secretary and treasurer; Gus. A. Davidson, chief clerk. Directors: Russell W. Harrison, S. Horace McKenzie, Hart H. Wade, Gus A. Davidson, J. P. Jetton.

The stock carried embraces a full, complete, and up-to-date line of dry goods, clothing, shoes, hats, notions, etc. They believe in a strictly cash system, and with such a system they have a rapidly growing business.

J. Freed.

J. Freed is a native of Prussia and was born in 1835. In 1854 he came to the United States and located in Columbus, Ga., where he remained until 1857, when he came to Memphis, Tenn., and embarked in the dry goods business. While there he joined the Washington Rifles, an old militia company. In 1860 he moved his stock of goods to Jackson, Tenn., where he remained till April, 1861, when being notified that Governor Harris called his company into service, he rejoined the company at Memphis. After doing two months' special duty, the company attached itself to the Fifteenth Tennessee Infantry, and took part in the battles of Belmont, Shiloh, Perryville, Murfreesboro, Chickamauga, Missionary Ridge, Resaca, Jonesboro, Dallas, Franklin, and Nashville, and he was wounded at Perryville, Chickamauga, and Dallas. He was captured in

J. FREED
(Merchant, Trenton).

front of Nashville in December, 1864, and was held as a prisoner of war six months.

In 1865 he settled in Trenton and engaged in the dry goods business. In 1874 he built his present storehouse and formed a copartnership with his brother-in-law, J. Ebert, which terminated with the death of Mr. Ebert in 1878. In 1893 he admitted his elder son, Henry, as a partner, under the firm name of J. Freed & Son. Henry, though still retaining an interest in his father's store, established in 1897, in connection with his cousin, Henry Ebert, a retail dry goods house at St. Louis, Mo.

In 1871 J. Freed married Miss Henrietta Cohn, who was also a native of Prussia. The marriage took place in St. Louis, Mo. This union has been blessed with thirteen children —ten boys and three girls; two of the boys died in infancy.

Mr. Freed is a member of the K. of P., K. of H., A. O. U. W., and is also a member of the Board of Aldermen of the city of Trenton.

Forked Deer Roller Mills, Trenton, Tenn.

This is one of the most important manufacturing industries of Trenton and of the county. The Forked Deer Roller Mills were established soon after the close of the Civil War by John L. Davis. J. H. Blakemore acquired an interest in the business, afterwards becoming sole owner. In 1882 the mill burned, and Mr. Blakemore disposed of the plant to R. N. Davis and D. E. Jetton, who rebuilt the mill.

In 1886 Mr. Jetton died, and J. W. Jetton and H. C. Pearce purchased the plant and put in the roller system in place of buhrs, with which the mill had been formerly equipped, completely remodeling and modernizing the plant.

In 1895 Mr. J. W. Jetton bought out his partner and became sole proprietor, and has since continued to operate it.

The plant is fitted with four sets of rollers and one corn buhr, and has a capacity of fifty-five barrels per day.

The Jetton family belongs to the pioneer settlers of Gibson County. The grandfather of J. W. Jetton, Isaac L. Jetton, came to Gibson County in 1822 and settled on a farm about three and a half miles west of Trenton, where he lived until his death in 1875. Robert Jetton, an uncle, was one of the commissioners appointed by the General Assembly of the State to locate the county seat, and he also, in conjunction with Solomon Shaw, built the courthouse in 1839-1840, which stood until the present structure was begun in 1899.

The present Mr. J. W. Jetton was born in Gibson County on a farm, and still carries on the farming business in connection with his mill. He and his family stand high in the social world of Trenton. Mrs. Jetton is the daughter of Judge Samuel Williams, who was Judge of the Gibson Circuit Court from 1858 to the breaking out of the Civil War.

Isaac L. Jetton.

Isaac L. Jetton was a pioneer settler of Gibson County. He was born in North Carolina

FORKED DEER ROLLER MILLS; JOHN W. JETTON, PROPRIETOR.

in 1799; moved to Rutherford County in 1803 and to Gibson County in 1822. He was a splendid type of the pioneer planter of the period—liberal, hospitable, living an easy,

ISAAC L. JETTON.

simple life; never working his negroes with a design of amassing wealth, but content to have a bountiful living for himself and his dependents.

D. E. Jetton.

D. E. Jetton, another of Gibson County's early settlers, was born near Murfreesboro, on August 24, 1818, and came to Gibson County in 1826. He was a prominent citizen

D. E. JETTON.

in the development of the county, and was the father of the present J. W. Jetton, of Trenton.

R. E. Grizzard.

Mr. R. E. Grizzard, head of one of the oldest business establishments in the city of Trenton, was born at Nashville on December 5, 1839. At the age of eleven he moved with his father to Tullahoma, Tenn., and came to Trenton in 1855, when only fifteen years old. He attended Andrew College and clerked in a store until 1858, when he rturned to Nashville. Here he clerked in a store until the breaking out of the war between the States, when he joined Company A, of Manny's First Tennessee Regiment. He was discharged from this regiment in 1862, serving the re-

R. E. GRIZZARD.

mainder of the war in the cavalry. He was paroled at Sumpterville, Ala., a member of Company A, Forrest's old regiment.

Returning to civil life, he clerked in the store of Senter & Biggs, and Biggs & Ellis, at Trenton for a time.

In 1872 he established his present hardware business, which he has continued down to the present time.

In 1869 Mr. Grizzard married Miss Clemenza Marshall, two daughters being born of this union—Mrs. Eliza McE. Rankin and Charlotte Virginia. Mr. Grizzard served a term as Mayor of Trenton in 1876, declining reëlection. In 1872 he joined the Presbyterian Church at Trenton, becoming one of its deacons, and later was ordained an elder, serving as such ever since. In 1869 he became a Mason and was Master of the Lodge at Trenton for many years.

After a life of remarkable usefulness, Mr. Grizzard died on August 8, 1901, mourned by the entire community.

Maj. William Gay.

Maj. Wm. Gay was born in Gibson County, Tenn., on January 22, 1827, and was reared and educated and remained a citizen of the county from the date of his birth to the time of his death. He was a merchant at Eaton for several years prior to the Civil War, but immediately upon the breaking out of the war he closed out his business and at once raised a company for the Confederate army, and when the company was organized he was elected its captain and was assigned to the Forty-seventh Tennessee Infantry. He served as captain of the company until the consolidation and reorganization at Corinth, when he was commissioned as captain to raise a company of cavalry. He came back home and soon had another company organized and ready for service, which was assigned to the Twentieth Tennessee Cavalry. He served his company as captain until 1864, when he was promoted and commissioned as major of his regiment, which position he held until the surrender.

As a soldier, Major Gay was always at his post and ready to do or die for his country's sake. In every engagement with the enemy he was always found in the forefront of the battle, leading and encouraging his men on to deeds of valor and heroism, and no better, braver, or more gallant officer ever bore a commission or unsheathed a sword. But when the surrender came and the old flag for the last time was furled, Major Gay, with his boys in gray, beat a slow but solemn retreat to his old home county, then made bare and desolate by the ravages of the war, and when he reached his old home he set about at once to build up the waste places and make his native county bloom and prosper as it did prior to the war.

For a few years after the war Major Gay sold goods in Trenton, but he soon sold out his stock of goods and retired to a farm and remained a farmer until his death.

In 1886 he was elected Trustee of Gibson County and reëlected in 1888, and as an officer he was honest and fearless, discharging every duty with promptness and fidelity, and it was frequently remarked during the term of his office that it was no difference whether he gave bond or not, for every cent of the public fund would be accounted for.

In 1865 Major Gay was married to Miss Mary E. Mays, who died on May 15, 1882. As the fruits of this marriage there were seven children, five of whom survive their father.

MAJ. WILLIAM GAY
(From a photograph taken just after the war).

He was a member of the Cumberland Presbyterian Church for nearly half a century and for many years an elder in said church and superintendent of its Sunday school, and in his church matters the same faithful, honest, intelligent discharge of duty characterized his every action. As a husband and father he guarded with the greatest care every want and interest of his family; as a neighbor he was clever and accommodating; as a public officer he was honest and watchful, as a church member he was diligent and faithful; as a soldier he was cautious, but brave; in times of peace he was a model citizen, and in time of war he was a brave and gallant soldier. In every walk of life he was honest, intelligent, industrious, faithful, and fearless.

Major Gay died after a short illness on March 21, 1901, regretted and mourned by all who knew him. For him life's trials and struggles are ended, and rest with the great Master whom he loved and served has been granted him with comrades who have preceded him to the land of rest.

> The muffled drum's sad roll has beat
> The soldier's last tattoo;
> No more on life's parade shall meet
> That brave and fallen few.
> On fame's eternal camping ground
> Their silent tents are spread,
> And glory guards, with solemn round,
> The bivouac of the dead.

The O. H. Strahl Bivouac, of which Major Gay was president, passed and ordered spread upon its minutes, the following resolution:

"Resolved, That in the death of Maj. Wm. Gay the Bivouac has lost a faithful and much beloved officer and member; the old Confederate veterans a true friend; the lost cause an ardent devotee; the State and county a most worthy and excellent citizen; the church a faithful, fearless, Christian member; and the family a kind, considerate, and loving father."

W. L. SMITH, DECEASED.

W. L. Smith, Deceased.

W. L. Smith was born in Wilson County in 1848. His younger days were spent in Agricultural pursuits, and at spare times he attended the neighborhood school. When yet quite a young man, he started out to make his own way in the world. His business education began in the town of Milan, where he first entered a mercantile house as a clerk. After remaining there for a while, he came to Trenton and began clerking for J. W. Hays, who at that time conducted the largest general retail store in Western Tennessee. Here Mr. Smith schooled himself for his successful struggle in after years. Imbibing all of the business sagacity of his employer and coupling it with his own natural abilities in this line, he fitted himself admirably for his future career. With the accumulations from the toil of his younger years he entered business for himself in connection with his brother, T. J. Smith, under the firm name of Smith Bros. For years this firm did an extensive dry goods and (for a portion of the time) grocery business at this place. They built the large two-story brick on the southwest corner of College street and Court Square, and these two commodious storerooms with basement gave them sufficient room for their rapidly increasing

SMITH BLOCK, CORNER COLLEGE STREET AND COURT SQUARE, TRENTON.

trade. Afterwards they extended the block on College street by the erection of three more elegant brick business houses.

In 1878 W. L. Smith was married to Miss Joe Hope, and only one child, a son, C. E. Smith, was born to them.

Mr. Smith accumulated considerable real estate in the city and county. The residence, Oak Manor, in which Mr. Smith lived for many years, is one of the most desirable residence sites in Trenton.

He was one of Trenton's most loyal and enterprising citizens. He loved the town and was ever ready to contribute his energies and his money to the town's upbuilding and to its general welfare.

A number of years after the closing out of the firm of Smith Bros. Mr. Smith embarked in business alone, and successfully conducted the same until the summer of 1899, when his failing health demanded his retirement.

In January, 1900, he, together with his family, moved to Berkeley, Cal., in search of recuperation, but he gradually grew worse and after fifteen months' residence in the West, returned to Trenton and died in this city on June 22, 1901, and was laid to rest in beautiful Oakland Cemetery.

His life and example are worthy of emulation, for, from an humble beginning, depending entirely upon his own resources, with energy and perseverance, he, in a few years, established himself as one of the most successful business men in Gibson County. He was a member of the Methodist Episcopal Church, South, and died in the hope of a blessed immortality.

The C. F. Smith Company.

The present business of the C. F. Smith Company is the oldest (or one of the oldest) business in the county. It was established in March, 1867, by C. F. Smith, deceased, who came to Trenton from Louisville, Ky. He opened a complete line of stoves, tinware, heavy hardware, agricultural implements, with tin, sheet iron and job work, etc. C. F. Smith continued in business until his death, which occurred on October 12, 1897. He was succeeded by a son, Leslie W. Smith, a daughter, Bertha M. Smith, and sister, Margaret Smith, who formed a copartnership under the name of C. F. Smith Co., with Leslie W.

LESLIE W. SMITH
(Of the C. F. Smith Company).

Smith as general manager. The latter, whose photo is given above, was born on September 26, 1872, and was well acquainted with the business when he took charge of it, having worked in the shop from childhood up.

Mr. Leslie W. Smith is regarded as one of the best citizens of Trenton, progressive in all respects and reliable and trustworthy in business life.

Trenton Saw and Planing Mill; Wade Bros. and Partee, Proprietors.

The Trenton Saw and Planing Mill is one of the important industries of Trenton, and the largest wood-working establishment in Trenton.

The works were established in 1885, but were not acquired by the present owners until 1899.

In 1899, W. L. Wade, H. L. Wade, and B. A. Partee bought the plant, which they enlarged and refitted, adding new machinery and improvements, making it entirely modern in all its various departments, and one of the most complete in the county.

The output of the mill consists of rough and dressed lumber, house building material and planing mill work of all kinds, ready for

THE BIGELOW HOTEL.

the builder's use. A department of the work is devoted to sawing tight barrel staves.

In addition to the sawmills connected with the Trenton mill, the firm operates a sawmill north of Trenton, cutting about 5,000 feet of lumber per day.

The transactions of this plant will exceed $35,000 per annum, and three-fourths of a million staves.

The Wade brothers are natives of Gibson County, their father having been born in that county, and their grandfather, Hillery Wade, being one of the pioneer settlers of Gibson County. Mr. Partee is also a native of the county, and is a descendant of one of the pioneer families.

The Bigelow Hotel.

The Bigelow Hotel is one of the main institutions of Trenton. It is operated upon the hospitable order. Everybody that enters its hospitable portals feels that he can throw off the restraints of conventionality and make himself at home, no matter whether he is going to stay an hour, a day, or a week. No red tape about the management; no credentials required. Of course a fellow must pay his bill, but he is glad to do this, after he has enjoyed the "creature comforts," always the best going. There's a good deal in a landlord, too. Some landlords are grum and immensely secretive in regard to things the traveling public want to know about; in a word, look and act as if they were entitled to your gratitude as well as your money for what they furnish you. Not so here. "Ask, and ye shall receive; knock, and it shall be opened unto you." The landlord of this hotel at Trenton is John W. Bigelow. Everybody likes him. He is everybody's friend, a noble specimen of the human kind. Don't make up your mind this is fulsome praise, promoted by some ax-grinding motive on my part, or paid for at a penny a line. It is pure truth, evolved from experience. If you are not contented to take my word for it, just come and investigate for yourself.

John W. Bigelow.

Here is a portrait of John W. Bigelow, a native of Gibson County, an old citizen of Trenton and one of nature's noblemen. I use this latter term advisedly and believe I can establish its correctness by the testimony of everybody in Gibson County (and out of it, too) that knows him. He has been in business at Trenton for a quarter of a century, and if he has an enemy in the town, I never saw or heard of him or her. I believe he is not a

JOHN W. BIGELOW.

member of any church, but he inclines to Methodism and is a regular attendant upon the worship of that denomination. So far as real human goodness is concerned, he will compare well with the best in any church.

I don't want to praise him too highly, as he is a modest man and I had some trouble in securing his picture for my sketches on account of his aversion to notoriety. But I must be pardoned for giving some faint expression of my esteem and admiration for the man; I cannot help it. I might say more about him—his unaffected goodness, his unfailing good humor, his companionableness, his promptitude, and reliability in social and business affairs; but I forbear, feeling like I hadn't said half of what every one knows to be true. Mr. Bigelow is a merchant of long standing in the town. He is also proprietor and landlord of the best hotel in the town,

where most of the traveling people stop, because they like him and like his hotel. Did you know that running a hotel or other business, successfully, is like the successful operation of the American army and navy? It depends largely on the man behind the gun.

Most anybody with capital can fix up a hotel and stand around and let it run itself, but a successful hotel—a hotel that people like to stop at—is the result of personal fitness for the job.

Now I guess I've said enough about Mr. Bigelow. Some people may say I'm a little too effusive in my talk about him. You notice I haven't said a word about his faults. I expect he has faults—everybody has—but I've not discovered them. If he has any, let those that know them speak.

T. Harlan & Co., Manufacturers and Dealers in Staves and Stave Timber.

This extensive industry has been in operation a number of years with headquarters at Trenton and has grown from small beginnings to be one of the most important enterprises of the city, contributing largely to its growth and prosperity.

The business of this firm in handling and manufacturing staves and stave material covers all of West Tennessee and its transactions aggregate a quarter of a million dollars per annum.

The firm of T. Harlan & Co. has been a very prosperous and successful one, notwithstanding it has had two very disastrous fires in its late history. In 1899 the firm sustained a loss by fire of $10,000 on machinery, buildings, and stock, and on June 25, of the following year, had another fire which consumed their mill, dryhouse, and a vast amount of finished stock, entailing a loss of $25,000.

But the firm, undaunted by these losses, are making arrangements to extend their operations and increase their facilities for manufacturing staves and handling stave material. The firm is composed of Mr. T. Harlan and Mr. Mac Morris, both of whom are splendid business men and highly esteemed citizens of Trenton.

Mr. Harlan is a man of family, whose ac-

PLANT OF TRENTON STAVE MILLS; T. HARLAN & CO., PROPRIETORS.

complished daughters move in Trenton's best social circles. Mr. Morris is unmarried, young, gallant, and a universal favorite in the social world of Trenton.

William Jarrell, Deceased.

William Jarrell was born in East Tennessee, but shortly afterwards his parents moved to the middle portion of the State, where he was reared. He came to Trenton in 1853, and worked at his trade of building cotton gins and stocking plows, the casting being bought of the well-known Avery Plow Works. In 1856 he built a foundry and machine shop here, which was the first manufacturing enterprise in the town or county, save a sawmill or two; and he erected and blew the first steam whistle ever blown in the county, as no railroads had at that time been built through here. In 1857 he sold an interest in the foundry to J. I. Wells and J. A. McDearmon, and with them continued the business until 1869, selling out to Mr. Wells at that time. In 1861 he obtained a patent on what is known as Jarrell's plow, which became universally used over the entire South. He was also the patentee of a cotton scraper, a cotton cleaner, two corn and cotton planters, and a nut lock.

After leaving Trenton, Mr. Jarrell built a foundry and flouring mill at Humboldt, which he operated for two years, after which

WILLIAM JARRELL, DECEASED
(Noted manufacturer, of Trenton, and inventor of the Jarrell Plow).

W. H. Dodson bought an interest, and it was conducted under the firm name of Jarrell & Dodson. This partnership continued until

1878, when he sold out his interest to Dodson and moved to Arkansas, where he opened a furniture store and purchased a farm twelve or fifteen miles from Fort Smith. Selling the furniture business, he finally retired to his farm.

Recently Mr. Jarrell sold his Arkansas property and moved to Smyrna, Middle Tennessee. He was for a while a Confederate soldier, and did more for Trenton and Gibson County in the early days of the county than any other man who ever resided within its bounds.

The Herald-Democrat.

One of the best county papers published in West Tennessee is the Herald-Democrat. The paper is Democratic in politics and is ably edited by Mr. Edward E. Benton, its owner. Mr. Benton makes his paper clear-cut, but not rabid, in handling the political issues of the day; but perhaps the most notable feature of the paper is its high moral tone and its devotion to county interests. This is the province of a county paper and Mr. Benton fully illustrates it in the conduct of his paper. Mr. Benton established the Gibson County Herald in 1885. In 1895 he purchased the Gibson County Democrat and consolidated the two papers under the title "Herald-Democrat." Mr. Benton is a member of the City Council and of the Board of Public Works of the city of Trenton; a member of the Methodist Church and one of the trustees of the church.

E. E. BENTON
(Editor Herald-Democrat).

INTERIOR VIEW OF MRS. J. G. SEDBERRY'S MILLINERY STORE, TRENTON, TENN.,
THE LEADING MILLINERY ESTABLISHMENT OF GIBSON COUNTY.

INTERIOR VIEW OF J. M. SKILES & CO.'S MAMMOTH DRY GOODS STORE, TRENTON.

J. M. Skiles & Co.

J. M. Skiles & Co., dry goods, clothing, shoes, hats, and variety goods such as are usually carried in a first-class dry goods store. Established in 1882 by J. M. Skiles. Southwest corner of Court Square and Eaton Street. Cheapest dry goods house in Gibson County.

John H. Parr.

Mr. John Hess Parr, to give his appellation in full, is the leading gentleman tailor as well as the leading gentlemen's tailor in Trenton, with a trade and business coextensive with the county. He is also an up-to-date "hustler" from a business standpoint and the best public crier and auctioneer in town. This comes of native talent and a disposition to make things go.

To use his own language, he has "hustled" for himself since he was fifteen years old. Socially, he is with the young set plucking gayly the flowers that spring by the pathway of life, but in business practical and pushing. He is, in fact, a large-hearted and generous-minded boy, impulsive in disposition, liable to err, but quick to own and correct a fault or mistake.

He belongs to one of the best families of the county and moves in the best social circles. With such social and business qualities, I shall look to see my young friend, Parr, become a distinguished business man and citizen as time adds to his length of days.

The town of Ripley, in which he has established himself in business, is to be congratulated in receiving him into its business and social circles.

JOHN H. PARR.

Henry N. Forrest.

Henry Nathan Forrest was born in Henry County, Tenn., in the year 1871. His father was a first cousin of Gen. N. B. Forrest. When two years old, he had a spell of fever, which resulted in total blindness. At the age of thirteen he entered the Tennessee School

HENRY N. FORREST
(Blind merchant of Trenton).

for the Blind, where he received a liberal literary and handicraft education. His father died in 1874, and his mother in 1885, leaving him homeless and without means. While at school, he earned his clothes and paid his way to and from Nashville by doing small jobs of work about the building. He completed the high school and Latin course and graduated with honors in May, 1892. He then returned to Henry County, and, having a desire to teach, took an examination under the county superintendent and received a first-grade certificate, which entitled him to teach anywhere in the county; but failing to secure a position as teacher, he worked on the farm, where he did almost any kind of work, except to plow. He finally succeeded in getting a broom machine and a small stock of material, and for a time he manufactured and sold brooms in the surrounding country.

In 1895 Mr. Forrest made the race for County Superintendent of Henry County, and was defeated by only a very small majority.

In July of the same year he moved to Trenton, and went into the manufacturing of brooms, associating with him in this work Messrs. Baker and Womble, two of his blind schoolmates. Mr. Forrest was traveling salesman for the concern, and did his work without the help of railroad conductors or hotel porters. Mr. Womble soon withdrew from the business, and in 1897 Mr. Forrest and Mr. Baker mutually agreed to dissolve partnership. He then opened a confectionery stand in the city of Trenton, which he still runs. He has succeeded fairly well, and owns a little building, known as the "City Stand," which he has fixed to his own notion. He does all his work except on busy days, when he hires some one to help him. He is attentive to his business, keeps it in good shape, is good for all his contracts, depends on no one but himself for support, and can go anywhere he wishes without a guide.

W. G. Smith, Deceased.

W. G. Smith was born in Middle Tennessee, and here his young manhood was spent. He learned the cabinetmaker's trade, and

W. G. SMITH, DECEASED.

worked in furniture factories at Nashville and other Middle Tennessee points. At an early age he professed religion and joined the old

Mill Creek Baptist Church, of that section, which has gained so much historical prominence.

At the beginning of the Civil War Mr. Smith moved to Trenton with his family, and was for a long time the only person in the place to do cabinet work, making coffins, and stocking guns. Shortly after the conflict closed he went into the furniture business, and for a number of years manufactured a large line of furniture and coffins at this place, working as high as twelve or fifteen men. He brought the first furniture to Trenton ever sold here from a manufactory. He remained in the furniture and undertaking business until his death, in 1898. For a long number of years he was one of the town's aldermen, and was ranger of the county for over thirty years. He was an ardent church member and member of the Trenton Masonic lodge. At his death Trenton lost one of her most trustworthy and exemplary citizens. He left a widow and two sons, John R. and Lon W. Smith.

John R. Smith.

John Robert Smith was born in Nashville, Tenn., on May 5, 1857, and moved with his parents to West Tennessee a year or so later. He was educated at Andrew College, Trenton, and for a number of years conducted his father's furniture business. The firm was finally styled John R. Smith & Co.

In 1882 Mr. Smith was elected Mayor of Trenton, and held that honorable position one term. For twenty years he was with the Evansville Coffin Company as their general Southern representative, and is now representing on the road the Ohio Valley Coffin Company. He is Past Master of Trenton Masonic Lodge, and has always taken a great interest in lodge matters. In 1899 he was chosen by the Grand Lodge Junior Grand Warden; in 1900 he was elected Senior Grand Warden; in 1901, Deputy Grand Master; and is in line to become Grand Master at the next meeting of the Grand Lodge. He was for eight years lecturer for the Ninth Congressional District for the Masonic Fraternity. He is a member of Kenton Chapter and Kenton Commandery, Knights Templar.

Mr. Smith has a beautiful home on High street, Trenton, and an interesting family, consisting of a wife and one child. He is genial and whole-souled, and is well known over the entire State and a large portion of the South.

J. W. Vick.

J. W. Vick is a native Tennessean and a native Gibson Countian, full of pride in his great State and enthusiastic over its great future. He is specially proud of his native county and her thrifty and intelligent people.

He was born in Gibson County on February 21, 1857, and has lived in the county all his life. He was reared on a farm, and knows the pleasures and hardships of life on a country farm, and he finds one of his chief pleasures now in the associations with the people from the country.

His parents were unable to give him the benefit of a higher education, and at first he had to content himself with the opportunities afforded by the neighborhood public schools.

At the age of fifteen he suffered a severe affliction. As the result of a protracted fever he had paralysis in one of his legs, and he has been compelled to go on crutches since that time. Full of ambition and energy, he was not daunted by this affliction, and continued at school, and at an early age began

JOHN R. SMITH
(Grand Lecturer of the State of Tennessee, F. and A. M.).

to teach school and go to school. He attended school at Bethel College, at McKenzie, and there fitted himself for a teacher in the public schools. He was a successful

J. W. VICK
(Clerk of the Circuit Court of Gibson County).

teacher, and in the school work he made a reputation and friends which have not failed him in after life.

In 1882 he was happily married, and after his marriage he continued to teach school.

In 1886 he became Democratic candidate for Clerk of the Circuit Court, and after a heated canvass, at one of the most exciting conventions ever held in Trenton, he received the nomination over five strong competitors. Since that time he has been three times elected to the same office without Democratic opposition. He is a fine canvasser, and knows how to mingle with the people; but the real cause of his success is his knowledge and sympathy with the great masses of the people.

He has made an excellent officer, and won the confidence and esteem of the people of his county. He is conservative, but firm in all matters, true to his friends and convictions.

He has a pleasant home in Trenton, where he enjoys the pleasure of an interesting family and the association of a pleasant community. He is a striking example of a successful country boy who has won his way in the face of poverty and affliction, backed only by pluck, energy, and good sense.

Gibson County Journal.

This newspaper has lately passed into the hands of Mr. W. H. Kerr, one of Gibson County's progressive farmers and fruit growers, who will no doubt conduct the paper in the interest of agriculture and for the promotion of the farming interests of the county. Mr. Kerr is a good business man, and will no doubt make a success of the paper.

Trenton Business Directory.

Agricultural Implements.—R. C. Adams, Freeman & Herbert, W. E. Birmingham, Phelan Brothers.

Bakers and Confectioners.—L. Metz, Butler & Co., Ebbert & Benson.

Banks.—Gibson County Bank, Exchange Bank.

Barbers.—Charles Allen, W. D. Sims, Duke Williams.

Blacksmith.—W. H. Wilson.

Clothing.—J. M. Skiles & Co., Harrison Dry Goods Company.

Dentists.—D. M. Haste, R. Harwood, —— Vansycle.

Druggists.—Lain Brothers, N. L. McRee, Leroy Shackelford, Famous.

Dry Goods.—Harrison Dry Goods Company, J. M. Skiles & Co., R. M. Davis, J. Freed, M. Fishman (general store), B. F. Jones (general store).

Furniture and Undertakers.—W. E. Seat, undertaker and funeral director of ten years' experience; also dealer in fine and cheap furniture, carpets, wall paper, window shades, and picture moldings. Satisfaction as to prices and services guaranteed. East Side Broadway, in Pythian Building. Adams Brothers.

Foundry.—B. F. Watson & Co.

Fruits.—H. N. Forrest.

Grocers.—J. W. Bigelow, R. C. Adams, J. A. Veazey, C. F. Givens, Syd Harrison, J. H. Blakemore, J. A. Landis, L. W. Moore, T. J. Adams, Ch. Prybass, J. H. Hefley, H. C. Gordon.

Hardware.—R. E. Grizzard, Phelan Brothers, R. C. Adams.

Hotels.—Bigelow Hotel, Solomon House, New Hicks House, Rogers House, Thomas House, Mrs. Harwood, private boarding.

Ice Factories.—Trenton Ice Factory and Bottling Works.

Jewelers.—G. S. Gardner & Co., H. G. Jones.

Lawyers.—James R. Deason, Quintan Rankin, Harry Elder, J. C. McDearmon, Yandell Haun, T. E. Harwood, L. H. Tyree, W. W. Wade, G. W. Wade, J. R. Walker, C. E. Hunt, T. J. Hays, R. P. Raines.

Laundries.—Trenton Steam Laundry.

Liverymen.—Henry Oppenheimer, Bud Lewis, S. V. Williams, E. C. Skiles.

Milliners.—Mrs. J. G. Sedberry, Miss Hattie Walker.

Meat Markets.—Conner & Pearce, D. R. Pursley.

Newspapers.—Herald - Democrat, Gibson County Journal.

Photographers.—Ben Oppenheimer.

Physicians.—T. J. Happel, J. T. Faucett, B. T. Bennett, D. A. Walker, J. M. Keys (colored).

Produce and Feed.—W. R. Duncan.

Saloons.—W. J. Barnett, D. F. Phelan, Lewis & Co., L. W. Cursey, P. J. Pybass.

Shoemakers.—A. W. Bigelow.

Saddlery.—J. H. Hefley, Freeman & Herbert.

Stoves and Tinware.—C. F. Smith Company.

Tailors.—A. Schneider, John Hess Parr.

Wagons and Buggies.—Freeman & Herbert, Phelan Brothers, W. E. Birmingham.

People of Gibson County Who Have Reached a Very Old Age.

Rev. A. J. Fletcher, of Rutherford, is the oldest person now living in the county who was born in the county. Maj. William Gay, who lately died, was the oldest. Mr. Fletcher was born in 1828. His father came to the county in 1822.

Mrs. Alethia Pope, who died near Rutherford on April 10 last, had the rare distinction of living partly in three centuries. She was born in the eighteenth, lived through the nineteenth, and died in the first year of the twentieth century. She was born in North Carolina in 1796, and came to Gibson County with her husband, Barney Pope, in 1840. Her husband died in 1862. Mrs. Pope was

MRS. ALETHIA POPE
(Who lived 105 years).

the mother of ten children, only one of whom, Mrs. Pearcy Cruse, is now living.

Aunt Penny Hartsfield is now ninety-seven years old. Mrs. Hartsfield was born in Wake County, N. C., on April 21, 1804. She married her husband, Richard Hartsfield, and removed to Tennessee in 1832. She lived in Maury County two years, and came to Gibson County and settled on a farm in the Fifth District on what was then called the Key-corner road, now the Trenton road, about three-quarters of a mile west of Brazil, where she has resided ever since. Her husband died in July, 1888 at the age of eighty-six. Mrs. Hartsfield is the mother of ten children, five of whom are living. She has many grandchildren and great grandchildren and one living great-great grandchild. She enjoys good health, and is quite active for her age. Her mental faculties are strong, and her recollection of early times is good. A few years ago she met with an accident which dislocated her hip, which incapacitates her somewhat; but otherwise she has good use of her body.

Rev. John Randall, still living near Trenton, was born in 1811. He is now past ninety. He began preaching in 1842. Mr. Randall was in the Creek and Seminole Wars, and has been prominent all his life as a preacher and in civil affairs. For several years past he has not preached on account of the infirmities of old age, but he still takes a lively interest in religious work.

CITY OF DYER.

This thriving little city is situated in the north middle portion of Gibson County, on the line of the Mobile and Ohio Railroad, 70 miles south of Cairo, 100 miles east of Memphis, 166 miles west of Nashville, and 310 miles south of Louisville.

The history of Dyer dates from the completion of the Mobile and Ohio Railroad through the county in 1858. This railroad established a station on the spot, the United States Postal Department established a post office, and the town of Dyer began its political, business, and social career. It received the name of Dyer as a sort of compliment to the county of Dyer, from whose productive soil and thrifty farmers its founders and projectors anticipated a strong support in developing the commerce of the place.

The town was laid off upon the lands of B. F. Bobbitt, a prominent and highly-respected citizen of the county, who was a merchant, and died in 1899.

The country around Dyer, both in Gibson and Dyer Counties, in point of fertility, is equal to any in West Tennessee. It is finely adapted to diversified farming, producing splendid crops of grain and grass, vegetables and fruit.

Since about 1888 the farmers about Dyer have entered largely into the culture of fruit, especially strawberries, producing and shipping in good seasons as high as 100 car loads of the latter fruit in a season. This fact has made Dyer famous as a center of the strawberry culture, no other single point in the strawberry zone of West Tennessee equaling her in the magnitude and value of this product. More than 1,000 acres are devoted to this product in the neighborhood, and in the picking season no less than 3,000 persons are given employment in saving the crop.

In the first stages of its history the growth of the town was slow, and the Civil War, coming on immediately after its founding, checked to a great extent the industrial and commercial development of the town.

In 1890 the population of Dyer was 600. The next decade witnessed a most phenomenal growth along all lines of improvement and development. The population increased to 1,200 in 1900. Business blocks had been erected, manufactories had been installed, many modern private residences had been built, a splendid school had been put in successful operation, several handsome church buildings had been built, and a wonderful spirit of progress became manifest in the entire people of the place.

CORPORATION OF DYER.

For municipal purposes the town is divided into four wards. The town government consists of a Mayor, Recorder, Marshal, night watchman, and eight aldermen (two from each ward). The present town officers are:

R. B. McDaniel, Mayor.
Henry D. Hays, Recorder.
W. J. Lawrence, Marshal.

Aldermen: First ward, J. M. Evans and W. A. Raines; second ward, W. J. Davidson and R. L. Crenshaw; third ward, C. O. Ewell and R. R. Kinton; fourth ward, J. W. Hopper and R. H. Hearn.

J. A. McLeod is a magistrate of the town, elected by the voters of the corporation, but is a member of the County Court.

The town has a good system of electric lights, owned by a private company. It gives good service. This plant is owned and operated by S. W. McCullar & Co., who installed the system in 1899. The company has about 500 private consumers in the town, besides the contract for lighting the streets. Twenty and thirty-two candle power lights are furnished consumers at an average cost of 45 cents per light per month.

The town is authorized by its charter to issue bonds for installing waterworks, but has not yet made a move toward making this improvement.

The religious and moral tone of Dyer is excellent. There are five churches, all flourishing and growing in numbers and influence. No intoxicants are sold in the town.

CHURCHES OF DYER.

Dyer Baptist Church.

This church was organized on December 27, 1885, with a membership of twenty-two. The congregation was organized in the Methodist house of worship, and continued to meet in same until the following year, when the present church building was erected. The first pastor was Rev. J. W. Gooch. The following pastors have served the congregation since: W. D. Haste, J. L. Dawes, W. H. Hughes, W. S. Roney, and T. A. Wagoner. The present pastor is W. A. Jordan, a graduate of the University at Jackson, formerly

REV. W. A. JORDAN
(Pastor Baptist Church, Dyer).

pastor of the church at Bolivar, Tenn. This is Mr. Jordan's second pastorate since he entered the ministry. His ministerial work has been most satisfactory in the charges he has filled.

The Sunday school of the church is a flourishing institution, with fifty scholars. Mr. J. H. Dement, one of Dyer's prominent citizens and business men, is the superintendent.

The church is now being remodeled and enlarged at an estimated cost of $400.

Methodist Church of Dyer.

The Methodist Episcopal Church, South, of Dyer, is one of the strongest and most influential religious organizations of the town. This church has a large and zealous member-

REV. W. W. ARMSTRONG
(Pastor Methodist Episcopal Church, South, Dyer).

ship, and is increasing its numbers rapidly under the pastorate of Rev. W. W. Armstrong. I have not been able to obtain a history of this church or the names of its officers.

Rev. T. J. Simmons is in charge of Dyer Circuit, consisting of the following churches:

Poplar Grove, three and one-half miles east of Dyer, was organized in 1850; has a present membership of 200.

Greer's Chapel, three miles south, was organized in 1890; has a membership of 75.

Good Hope, three miles west, has a membership of 110.

Hopewell, six miles west, has a membership of 115.

The Cumberland Presbyterian Church of Dyer

has a good brick church building and the greatest number of communicants of any church in Dyer. The membership of this church is about 200. Rev. J. B. Waggoner is pastor.

The Christian Church

of Dyer has about 50 members. This church has a growing congregation, and some of the best citizens of Dyer and the country adjacent are in its membership. The congregation are taking steps to build a new house of worship.

EDUCATIONAL AND BUSINESS INTERESTS OF DYER.

West Tennessee College.

This institution is one of the best in the county. It has a large and commodious college building, well furnished, and equipped with all the appliances for successful teaching. It has a commanding situation on elevated ground, overlooking the town. The college has a high reputation for thoroughness in the training of youth in all the essentials that enter into the character of the useful citizen.

The president of the school, Mr. James A. Tate, has had large experience in the training and education of children, and is a strong believer in character building as well as in intellectual culture. Hence the youth intrusted to his care are instructed and taught that the development of the moral nature is of equal importance with that of the intellectual.

The course of study in this school embraces the eight statutory grades in which the pupils of the school district are enrolled to the number of 400. This department is free to the children of the town and school district. Pupils outside of the district pay for tuition.

The full college curriculum embraces a scientific and classical course of study, which fits the pupil for graduation with the B.S. degree.

Instruction in music and bookkeeping are special features of the college.

My space will not admit of a detailed statement of course of study and school management in West Tennessee College. Persons desirous of information on these subjects are referred to Mr. James A. Tate, president of the college faculty, who will answer all inquiries. The faculty of the college is as follows:

James A. Tate, A.M., President
Mrs. L. L. C. Tate, A.M., English and Literature.
John F. Smith, B.S., Latin, Greek, and Science.
Frank N. Johnson, A.B., Collegiate Department.
King A. Hagy, A.B., Academic Department.
Clara L. Anderson, Primary Department.
Sarah L. Belcher, Music Department.

Board of Trustees:
W. S. Coulter, President.
J. H. Dement, Secretary.
J. A. Jackson.
J. W. Davidson.
J. Y. Mitchell.
R. R. Kinton.
R. B. McDaniel.
W. J. Davidson.
A. M. Kelly.

RESIDENCE OF G. W. FARRIS, HARDWARE AND FARM IMPLEMENTS, DYER.

The Farmers and Merchants' Bank of Dyer

was organized and incorporated under the general laws of the State in 1895. It has had a most prosperous career in business since its organization, and has contributed greatly to the development of the business interests of Dyer. Its officers are all wide-awake, progressive men, giving aid and support to Dyer enterprises and encouragement to every movement for building up the town as a business center. It has a subscribed capital of $34,000, of which $17,000 is paid in. Its surplus and profit account reaches $2,500. It has paid a semiannual dividend of five per cent since its organization. The officers of the bank are:

C. O. Ewell, President.
J. W. Davidson and S. W. McCullar, Vice Presidents.
Russell Dance, Cashier.
W. T. Becton, Bookkeeper.

Dyer Fruit Box Manufacturing Company.

This is one of the most thriving and important industries of the county, and exhibits in a marked degree the enterprise of the people and the growth and development of the fruit culture in West Tennessee. The plant was established in 1889, and incorporated under the general laws of the State in that year.

The cost of the plant, with its entire equipment, as it stands to-day, represents a value of $10,000.

The plant consists of a main sawing and cutting mill, fitted with the latest modern machinery and appliances for getting out box material; two large warerooms, 30x130 feet, for storage of finished work; two dry sheds, 30x200 feet, all together covering some two and three-quarter acres of ground.

The plant is lighted by its own system of electric lights.

It is immediately on the main line of the Mobile and Ohio Railroad, with ample switching tracks for receiving and shipping purposes.

The output of the mill for 1890, which is the last accessible report of its product, was ninety-one car loads of finished work.

In addition to a market and demand for the product of the factory in outside fruit-growing sections, there is an immense home trade, the plant being situated in one of the best fruit-producing regions of the country.

The factory employs some thirty-five adults, and its pay roll will average for most of the year $200 per week.

RESIDENCE OF R. B. M'DANIEL, OF THE FIRM OF HEARN, M'DANIEL & CO., CONTRACTORS AND BUILDERS, DYER.

The management of this industry is in the hands of C. O. Ewell, general manager, who attends to all of its affairs.

Hearn, McDaniel & Co., Contractors and Builders, and Proprietors of Dyer Planing Mill.

The history of this plant dates from 1891. In that year Mr. R. H. Hearn opened and operated a lumber yard and carried on the business of contracting and building in Dyer, following the same until 1895. In that year he established the planing mill, equipping the same with modern machinery, and organized the present company by taking in as associates in the business R. B. McDaniel, J. C. Hearn, and G. W. Hearn. This firm has done a very large business in Dyer and vicinity.

Mr. Hearn informs me that since he began business the firm has built complete more than two hundred houses, besides doing the wood work for most of the brick buildings in the town and adjacent country. In fact, this firm has nearly a monopoly of the building business in and about Dyer.

The members composing the firm of Hearn, McDaniel & Co. are all prominent citizens, taking an active and useful part in public affairs as well as in the social welfare of the community. Mr. R. B. McDaniel is Mayor of the town, and Mr. R. H. Hearn is one of its aldermen.

Dyer as a Produce Market.

Dyer is the largest market for the handling of poultry and eggs in Gibson County. Over fifty car loads of poultry (200,000 head) are shipped from this point per annum, with an increasing market supply. Over ninety-six thousand dozen (1,152,000) eggs were handled here last season by one firm. Messrs. Davidson & Crenshaw handle the major part of the shipments from this point, and are the largest dealers in these products in the county. Their business extends throughout Gibson County and adjoining counties and North Mississippi. This firm handles farm products generally, and its transactions in corn, wheat, potatoes, peas, strawberries, and fruits will aggregate a volume of trade exceeding $100,000 per annum. The firm was established in 1896, and, with a constantly increasing business, has become noted in West Tennessee.

Dyer Milling Company.

This enterprise is owned and operated by T. W. Owen and W. S. Coulter. Mr. T. W. Owen is manager. The mill was built in 1897 by a company composed of the present owners and W. T. Medling and J. H. Dement. Messrs. Owen and Coulter bought out the other proprietors in January, 1900.

The plant consists of a three-story brick building, with brick boiler and engine room

RESIDENCE OF J. H. DEMENT, PROMINENT MERCHANT OF DYER.

and warehouse. The mill is equipped with modern machinery throughout; has four double stands of rollers for wheat and one for corn, with a capacity of sixty barrels of flour per day.

Farris & Brooks, Dealers in Hardware, Stoves, Farm Implements and Farm Machinery, Wagons, Buggies, Pumps, Etc. Established in 1899.

G. W. Farris and L. M. Brooks, both natives of McNairy County, have been in business in Gibson County three years. They are agents for Plano mowers and binders. They handle the Harrison wagon, made at Grand Rapids, Mich.; Gestring wagon and New Hickory, both made at St. Louis. They have a large and growing trade.

Kerr, Davidson & Co., Manufacturers of Heading and Chair Backs.

This plant was established in February, 1900. The output of the factory per annum is about fifty car loads of heading and chair backs. The factory gives employment to fifteen people.

C. O. Ewell, S. W. McCullar, L. L. Davidson, and T. O. Kerr constitute the company operating these works. Mr. T. O. Kerr is manager.

The Dyer Reporter.

This newspaper is a live, bright, newsy sheet well worthy the progressive town whose cause it champions so ably. It was established under its present name in November, 1896, by B. W. Overall, who changed the name of the paper, which had been previously run as a Populist paper. For a year it was conducted as an independent paper, and then converted into a Democratic organ. In September, 1900, the Reporter was purchased by C. W. Cornforth, its politics being independent. In May of this year the paper was purchased by Messrs. Frank Lee and Thomas Kelly, and is now published by Lee & Kelly. These gentlemen are both good newspaper men, and are making the Reporter a strong factor in Dyer's business and social circles.

DEMENT BLOCK, DYER.

Business Directory of Dyer.

Agricultural Implements, Hardware, Buggies, Etc.—Farris & Brooks, J. H. Dement.
Banks.—Farmers and Merchants'.
Barbers.—J. T. Vestal, Joseph Davidson.
Blacksmiths.—J. T. Aspray.
Brickmakers.—J. F. Baulch.
Books and Stationery.—E. W. Gladhill.
Contractors.—Hearn-McDaniel Company, H. J. Craven.
Cotton Gins.—J. W. Baird & Co.
Confectioners.—McHugh & Parr, T. O. Kerr.
Dry Goods.—J. Y. Mitchell; Meade, Gordon & Davidson; J. W. Wilson, Johnston Mercantile Company, J. H. Dement, Jones & Son, S. H. Russell, W. J. Davidson, G. W. Robinson, Robinson & Flowers.
Druggists.—J. M. Evans, R. L. Dement.
Flouring Mills.—Dyer Milling Company.
Furniture and Undertakers.—J. W. Hopper & Co.

Groceries.—J. H. Dement, D. C. Foster, J. M. Watkins, T. O. Kerr, R. D. Kinton & Son, W. L. Baldridge, L. A. Richmond, Coulter & Berry, Grier Brothers.
Hotels.—Dyer Hotel, J. T. Boyd Hotel, J. K. Hathaway Hotel.
Hardware.—J. H. Dement, Farris & Brooks.
Insurance.—H. D. Hays, Farmers and Merchants' Bank.
Ice Dealers.—W. L. Baldridge.
Jewelers.—E. W. Gladhill.
Laundries.—White Star Rose.
Lawyers.—W. S. Coulter, W. D. Hayes.
Liverymen.—J. W. Davidson, Davidson & Berry.
Milliners.—Mrs. A. Robinson, Miss Eva Dickson.
Physicians.—J. A. Jackson, J. H. Drane.
Photographers.—Mrs. Frank Lee.
Produce Dealers.—Davidson & Crenshaw.
Sawmills.—J. W. Owens & Co.
Seed Cleaners.—Dixie Manufacturing Company.
Sale and Feed Stables.—A. J. Thornton.
Shoemakers.—R. H. Nanney.
Variety Stores.—J. C. Bruce, 5 and 10-cent store.

RESIDENCE OF DR. J. A. JACKSON, A LEADING PHYSICIAN OF DYER.

GIBSON COUNTY OF TO-DAY (Continued).

N. B. Johnson

was born in Maury County, Tenn., in 1841. He was reared on a farm, and has been a farmer all his life. He came to Gibson County in 1857, and settled in the Twenty-third District, about twelve miles north of Trenton, where he has resided ever since. He married Miss Lillie Taliaferro, of Weakley County, in 1865.

He served in the Confederate Army, Forty-seventh Tennessee Infantry, until the evacuation of Corinth by the Confederate forces in 1863, when he was discharged from the service on account of disability. After he left the service he devoted himself to farm pursuits.

In 1870 he was elected a magistrate in his district, and, with the exception of an interval of about two months, has served continuously as such ever since, being reëlected from time to time. During his incumbency of the magistrate's office, as a member of the County Court, he has been one of the progressive, active members of that body, advocating and supporting all measures for the advancement of the public welfare. He was strong in his support of the movement which resulted in the building of the splendid new courthouse.

Mr. Johnson is the oldest magistrate on the County Court bench, having been in service over thirty years. He is a man of clear perception and most reliable character in both

N. B. JOHNSON
(Member of County Court, Twenty-third District).

public and private life, and is highly esteemed for his personal worth and virtues. He is a member of the Masonic fraternity, and he and his wife are members of the Methodist Episcopal Church, South.

Hon. A. J. Collinsworth.

Hon. A. J. Collinsworth was born on the farm which he now owns and lives on, near Humboldt, in Gibson County, Tenn., on February 6, 1844. He worked on the farm and attended the district school, near by, until the outbreak of the war, and at the age of seventeen he entered the army, joining Capt. Jesse L. Branch's company, at this place, and then the Forty-seventh Tennessee Regiment, at Trenton, commanded by Col. M. R. Hill. He served in the war with the distinction of being one of the bravest boys and hardest fighters in the service. He was severely wounded in what was known as the hardest picket fight during the war at Corinth, Miss., by a minie ball, which shattered his leg, and from which he has never fully recovered.

After the war he returned home, to find his two older and only brothers dead and the farm gone to pieces. He at once set to work, and in a few years the farm was made to produce plentifully; but the war had cut him off from an education, which he very much desired. So he, with a great deal of pluck and determination to gain a good education, again entered school, and remained until he received a good common-school education. After this he again commenced work on his father's farm, where he remained until his twenty-seventh year, when he married Ella Robertson, near Trenton, and from this union he has five sons living, one of whom was in the First Tennessee Regiment during the Spanish-American War, and served as quar-

HEARN BLOCK, DYER.

termaster of his company while in the Philippines. Another son is now a member of the Twenty-third United States Infantry, and is serving in the Philippines.

HON. A. J. COLLINSWORTH.

After his marriage he continued to farm, and in 1872 he was cut off from Gibson County into the new county of Crockett, he being one of the organizers of that county. As soon as the county was organized he was elected constable, and also appointed deputy sheriff. He served in these two offices for the term of six years, when he was elected sheriff of the county. He then left the farm and moved to Alamo, where he served as sheriff for four years; and at the end of the second term he moved back to his farm, where he has since resided.

In 1884 he lost his wife, and in 1886 he was again married, this time to Bettie Raines, who was a daughter of E. B. Raines, a prominent farmer. By this union he has two sons and one daughter living.

Colonel Collinsworth was many years ago elected magistrate for his county, and has served in this office continuously since that time.

In 1896 he was elected to the State Senate from the district composed of Gibson and Crockett Counties by the largest plurality of votes ever cast in any election held in this district; and, besides this, he had probably the strongest man in Crockett County as his opponent. He served in our Fiftieth General Assembly as Senator with distinction, having been made chairman of the Senate caucus, and also serving on the most important committees. In fact, he filled the office with as much, or more, credit and distinction to himself and office than any Senator ever elected from this district.

He is a consistent member of the Methodist Episcopal Church, South; and is also an active member of two secret orders, the Knights of Honor and the Golden Cross.

The subject of this sketch was reared a poor boy, but by hard work and enterprise he has accumulated a small fortune, holding a large property interest in many parts of the country. He is, beyond a doubt, one of the most enterprising farmers in the State. Colonel Collinsworth is widely known, and there is scarcely a business enterprise of any description in our county that he is not connected with. It can truly be said that Colonel Collinsworth is a self-made man and has made a success in everything he has undertaken.

Prof. A. D. Hassell.

Prof. A. D. Hassell, whose portrait appears herewith, is the son of a farmer, his boyhood days having been spent in agricultural pursuits, five miles east of Trenton, Gibson County, Tenn. After attending school at Sylvan Dale, Trenton, and Humboldt, he

PROF. A. D. HASSELL.

taught for a few years, after which he spent three years in M. C. I., graduating in 1895. He was principal of the Eldad public school, this county, for five years, giving the utmost satisfaction and endearing himself to the hearts of the patrons and pupils alike.

For the spring term of 1899 he accepted a position in Bethel College, McKenzie, Tenn., teaching in the special teachers' department, and also taking a special course in that college.

During the 1901 vacation he had the honor of being appointed by the State Superintendent of Public Instruction to conduct a flourishing teachers' institute at Tracy City, Tenn., during the early part of the summer, and won some very flattering testimonials from those interested, besides the excellent complimentary notices from the Tracy City press, which, among other nice things, said: "Prof. A. D. Hassell, of Gibson County, has been assisting with the work of our county institute this week, and has entirely endeared himself to the teachers and our citizens generally, not only because of his thorough equipment as an educator, but for his genial social qualities as well."

Professor Hassell has so conducted himself at home and abroad as to possess some very strong and complimentary recommendations from many gentlemen of high standing and great influence. His scholarly attainments, moral character, and Christian conduct are such as to commend him to the favorable consideration of all who are interested in true educational effort. He takes a deep interest in everything pertaining to the upbuilding of the educational department of our State; and although yet quite a young man, he ranks among the leading educators of the Commonwealth.

Lands of Gibson County.

Some idea of the state of improvement and productiveness of the lands of Gibson County may be obtained by a study of the values placed upon them for purposes of taxation. The following table shows the average value of the lands in the different civil districts as exhibited by the assessor's books. The average assessed value of lands in the whole county, as we have seen in a former article, is $9.38 per acre. The values below are given in whole numbers:

District No.	1	$ 9
"	" 2	9
"	" 3	10
"	" 4	8
"	" 5	9
"	" 6	6
"	" 7	11
"	" 8	10
"	" 9	11
"	" 10	11
"	" 11	10
"	" 12	7
"	" 13	10
"	" 14	8
"	" 15	6
"	" 16	8
"	" 17	6
"	" 18	10
"	" 19	8
"	" 20	11
"	" 21	12
"	" 22	6
"	" 23	8
"	" 24	13
"	" 25	10

It will be seen from these figures that there is a wide difference in the range of values placed upon the lands in the different districts, indicating, no doubt, advantage of location, state of improvement, and productiveness. For instance, lands in the Twenty-first and Twenty-fourth Districts are valued twice as high as those in the Sixth, Fifteenth, Seventeenth, and Twenty-second Districts. The Twenty-fourth District bears rather a unique reputation. It is not only the acknowledged leader of all the other districts of the county in productiveness and agricultural progress, but it is singular in the fact that no negroes are allowed in the district. No negroes live or are employed in the district. Only white labor is tolerated, and almost every farmer owns his own land and cultivates his own farm.

I spent several days among the farmers of the Twenty-fourth District, and found them to be industrious, intelligent, moral, and exceptionally hospitable. Every man's latchstring was on the outer door, and his heart and hand were ready to welcome the stranger. There is no town in the Twenty-fourth District, but there are plenty of churches and schoolhouses. Religion and education are governing factors in the social life of the people. Some of the farmers whom I met are: W. T. Dement, W. A. Minton, L. C. Tomlinson, M. D. Ratladge, J. W. Jones, Dr. W. B. Duncan, Esq. J. Q. Temple, William Tilghman, Esq. John W. Hart, J. H. Hundley, James F. Herndon, Horace Graves, Bud Fisher, A. K. Harget, James Barton, Jesse Garner, Thomas Howell, D. Hedden, Henry Jones, J. E. Jones, and many others too numerous to mention.

There are few farms for sale in the Twenty-fourth District, and where lands change hands the price ranges from $20 to $50 per acre.

Statement of Shipments in Gibson County.

An an index of the resources and agricultural possibilities of Gibson County I present the following exhibit of shipments of farm and other products per annum from stations on the Louisville and Nashville, the Mobile and Ohio, and the Illinois Central Railroads, as compiled from the books of the local agents of these roads in the county. These figures are averaged from the transactions of the last five years:

Humboldt, Mobile and Ohio Railroad:

Strawberries	45	cars
Tomatoes and vegetables	32	"
Live stock	60	"
Grain	7	"
Potatoes	10	"
Peas	6	"
Poultry	2	"
Box material	80	"
Logs	45	"
Lumber	24	"
Staves	45	"
Spokes	25	"
Marble monuments	12	"
Plows	10	"
Nursery stock	30	"
Heading and hoops	13	"
Miscellaneous	12	"
Cotton bales	575	"

Humboldt, Louisville and Nashville Railroad:

Strawberries	55	cars
Tomatoes, vegetables, and fruit	90	"
Live stock	75	"
Grain	10	"
Poultry and eggs	5	"
Box material	84	"
Staves	50	"
Spokes	33	"
Lumber and logs	25	"
Heading and hoops	20	"
Marble monuments	20	"
Nursery stock	70	"
Plows	10	"
Cotton bales	400	"

Fruitland, Mobile and Ohio Railroad:

Strawberries	23	cars
Tomatoes	52	"
Fruit — peaches, apples, plums, pears, etc.	12	"
Cantaloupes	10	"
Live stock, grain, etc.	5	"
Miscellaneous	5	"

Trenton, Mobile and Ohio Railroad:

Live stock	125	cars
Grain	30	"
Flouring mill products	75	"
Fruit (orchard)	10	"
Poultry	5	"
Staves	900	"
Lumber	100	"
Logs	60	"
Cotton seed meal and oil	50	"
Peas, sorghum, potatoes, etc.	20	"
Cotton bales	3000	"

Dyer, Mobile and Ohio Railroad:

Strawberries	100	cars
Potatoes	52	"
Grain	66	"
Vegetables and fruits	25	"
Flour and bran	9	"
Poultry and eggs	58	"
Box material	76	"
Lumber and spokes	21	"
Miscellaneous	15	"
Cotton bales	546	"

Rutherford, Mobile and Ohio Railroad:

Grain	90 cars
Strawberries	35 "
Vegetables and orchard fruits	20 "
Peas	8 "
Poultry and eggs	10 "
Live stock	37 "
Logs, lumber, and staves	410 "
Flour and bran	75 "
Miscellaneous	20 "
Cotton bales	400 "

Milan, Louisville and Nashville and Illinois Central Railroads:

Strawberries	20 cars
Orchard products	30 "
Tomatoes and vegetables	18 "
Peas	22 "
Cotton seed, sorghum, etc.	40 "
Live stock	100 "
Poultry and eggs	5 "
Mill products	100 "
Grain	10 "
Staves	80 "
Cotton bales	3300 "

Medina, Illinois Central Railroad:

Strawberries	75 cars
Tomatoes	25 "
Vegetables and orchard products	25 "
Grain	12 "
Poultry and eggs	5 "
Lumber, logs, and staves	90 "
Cotton bales	600 "

Gibson Station, Louisville and Nashville Railroad:

Strawberries	50 cars
Tomatoes	150 "
Cabbage	10 "
Vegetables and orchard fruits	10 "
Poultry and eggs	10 "
Cotton bales	150 "

Bradford, Illinois Central Railroad:

Strawberries	30 cars
Tomatoes	75 "
Vegetables and orchard fruits	25 "
Peas	15 "
Live stock	25 "
Poultry	150 "
Cotton seed	24 "
Timber products	800 "

Ancient History, Traditional and Otherwise.

At the second term of the Circuit Court, held in the county on November 22, 1824, David Crockett was fined $25, as was also Yarnell Reese, for failing to obey the sheriff's summons as jurors. The fine of Yarnell Reese was remitted at the May term, 1825, and that of David Crockett at the November term following. The grand jury of the November term, 1824, was dismissed without finding any indictments. Presentments for violation of law at this time were principally for gaming.

The first divorce suit instituted in the county was William D. Lewis vs. Sarah Lewis at the fall term of the Circuit Court, 1826. The suit was dismissed. Afterwards, at the October term, 1830, on petition of Sarah Lewis, she was granted a divorce. At this term Green B. Chambers was presented for the murder of James Ricketts. The case was ordered dismissed by the court as not supported by reasonable cause.

Publication of nonresident notices were made in the Jackson Gazette, there being no newspaper published in Gibson County.

At the November term, 1825, of the Circuit Court, held at Gibsonport, the grand jury returned true bills for gaming against Robert Gray, John Gray, Bernard Adcock, and Joseph Curtis.

The first grand jury impaneled in the county was at the first term of the Circuit Court, held at the house of William C. Love, Judge John C. Hamilton presiding, and consisted of W. B. G. Killingsworth, foreman; Robert Beard, Isham T. Davis, George F. Crafton, William McKendrick, William W. Craig, Robert Temple, Robert Edmonson, John Spencer, Benjamin White, William Blakemore, Andrew Cole, and John Parker.

At the October term, 1825, of the County Court, John B. Hogg, John P. Thomas, Robert Tinkle, William C. Love, and John W. Evans were allowed $67 each for services as commissioners of the town of Gibsonport in laying off and selling the lots of the town.

In 1826 there were six persons in the county assessed with 5,000 acres of land each, as follows: Martin Armstrong, Jones & Bennett, George W. Gibbs, William Polk, Isaac

Roberts, and Thomas Travis, each of whom paid $43.75 taxes.

From the first settlement of the county up to the day of railroads the principal shipping point was Hickman, on the Mississippi River. Considerable shipping was done from Eaton, on Forked Deer River. Wagons were the means of transportation, and teaming was a regular business. The distance to Hickman from the county seat was about sixty miles. Hale's Point, at the mouth of Forked Deer River, was the transfer point for keel boats coming out of Forked Deer River. The cost of wagon transportation to Hickman was $2 per bale of cotton.

The contractors who built the brick courthouse in 1840-1 were Robert Jetton and Solomon Shaw. They also erected a building for the Branch Bank of Tennessee on the southwest corner of Public Square and Eaton street, Trenton.

The first marriage solemnized in the county was that of Richard Lewis to Sarah Sellers. The license was obtained from Stewart County. I wonder if this is the same couple who figured in the first divorce suit brought in the county? They were married in 1822. The court records give the names of the parties to the divorce suit as William D. Lewis vs. Sarah Lewis in 1826. Sarah was granted a divorce in 1830.

The first legal hanging in the county was that of a negro named Henry for murder of a boy, the son of a widow lady named Franklin. He was hanged at Trenton on April 4, 1843.

The first person sent to the penitentiary from Gibson County was Thomas Watson in 1835. He was sent for three years for horse stealing.

Some of the early lawyers of the county were the two Tottens, Felix Parker, Felix Grundy, R. P. Raines, Adam Huntsman.

Some of the early doctors were: Dr. Crisp, Dr. Fonville, N. I. Hess, Dr. Love, Dr. Lea, and Dr. Levy.

Some of the early merchants were: Robert Seat, Nelson Caruthers, Brown & Taliaferro, Woodfin & Elder Brothers, Claiborne & Davis, A. P. Griggsby, Seat & Norton.

The first mill for grinding corn was built by Thomas Fite and James Randolph on Forked Deer River. Soon after another mill was erected by Mr. Page on the same river, about ten miles west of Trenton. A Mr. Moore erected another mill in the same neighborhood, which was the first mill that ground wheat.

FRUITLAND

is a station and village on the Mobile and Ohio Railroad, five miles north of Humboldt. It is the center of a fine farming section, in the Twentieth Civil District, noted for the production of fruits and vegetables. Strawberry and tomato culture is carried on extensively by the farmers of this section, no less than thirty car loads of the former and sixty of the latter being shipped from this point in a season. Apples, peaches, pears, plums, and canteloupes enter largely into the sum total of shipments from Fruitland. Including all products, the annual shipments from this point will exceed 150 car loads.

The neighborhood of which Fruitland forms the trading and shipping center is noted for its high state of progress in industrial and social development. Religion, morals, and education are characteristic of the community. The Baptist, Methodist, Presbyterian, and Christian denominations, all have good church buildings and flourishing congregations. A splendid graded school is maintained, whose reputation for thorough educational work is known all over the county.

Edison Institute.

Edison Institute is beautifully located about two miles west of Fruitland at the crossing of the Poplar Corner and the Brazil and Fruitland roads.

This is a district public school that takes, on account of its magnitude and method of management, somewhat the character of a higher educational institution. The entire district is consolidated in this one institution. This enables the district to have an eight-months' school term and facilitates the maintenance of higher grades. In addition to the eight grades of the State curriculum, two grades in the high school are taught.

The school perhaps reached the highest enrollment under Prof. C. S. Henning, in 1897, when it reached the number of 147. The enrollment for the past year was 115. For the the past two years the school has been under the management of Miss Essie Mai Davidson as principal, with Miss Mattie Boyd in charge of the primary department and Miss Gertrude Fullerton in charge of the musical department.

MISS ESSIE MAI DAVIDSON
(Principal Edison Institute).

The school has been run entirely with public money, the public funds having never been supplemented by any private subscriptions of any kind. Much of the success of the school at Edison Institute is due to the careful, efficient method of management of the present board of directors, the present board having served for a number of years. The board of directors are: S. Mitchell, President; J. H. Koffman, Secretary; A. W. Freeman.

J. H. Koffman.

J. H. Koffman is of German descent and is a native of McNairy County, Tenn., but moved with his father to Gibson County when about ten years old. He is the third and youngest son of J. C. Koffman, who was born in Greene County, Tenn., but came to West Tennessee with his father when but a youth, and is still living. J. H. Koffman's mother was Abigail Hawkins Atkins, and was born in North Carolina about 1818. She died in 1898.

Mr. Koffman has always lived on a farm and been fully identified with the farming interests. His farm and home is situated five miles south of Trenton in the Twentieth District. He has always taken an active part in farmers' organizations; was for seven years secretary and treasurer of the Agricultural Wheel and Farmers and Laborers' Union of Gibson County, and was for a time secretary and treasurer of the Ninth Congressional District Farmers and Laborers' Union, and is at present secretary of the Gibson County Farmers' Institute.

He was educated principally at the Central Normal School and I. O. O. F. College at Humboldt, Tenn. After leaving school he taught in the public schools of the county for eight or ten years and was quite successful as a teacher. He has always taken great inter-

J. H. KOFFMAN
(Magistrate in Twentieth District).

est in educational matters and has served his district for a number of years as director, and is at present secretary of the board.

Mr. Koffman has at several times been engaged in the newspaper business of Gibson County, his first venture being in 1882 with the West Tennessee Argus, of Humboldt, of which he was for a time editor. In 1893 he established the Tennessee Populist, of which he was editor until he sold his outfit two years later. He is at present editor of the Gibson County Journal, published at Trenton. In addition to his editorial work he has contributed considerably to other papers and periodicals. He has twice been a candidate for State Senator; once as an independent candidate from Gibson County, and once as the nominee of the Populist party from the counties of Gibson and Crockett. In both of these races he made an active canvass and received a flattering support. In 1888 he was elected magistrate of his district, which office he has held continuously since, the present term to which he has been elected expiring in 1906.

Mr. Koffman was first married to Miss Emma B. Phelan in 1885. By this union three children were born, two boys and one girl—all living. His second marriage was April 7, 1901, to Miss Mattie L. Boyd, one of the most prominent primary teachers of the county.

Mr. Koffman is a member of the Baptist Church, his membership being at Center Church, where it has been for more than twenty-five years.

Mrs. J. H. Koffman.

Mrs. Mattie Boyd Koffman is a daughter of Mr. and Mrs. J. T. Boyd, of Dyer, Gibson County, Tenn. She was educated principally in the schools of Dyer and Rutherford. Since leaving school she has spent most of her time in teaching, having taught her first school at Rutherford. After teaching for three years she attended Bethel College, McKenzie, Tenn., in 1898, and took a teachers' training course, acquitting herself with honor. In the winter of 1898 she taught school at Locust Grove, in the Twenty-fourth District of this county, and the following year took charge of the primary department of Edison Institute, where she has been since. She has been for some time recognized as one of the county's leading primary teachers. On April 7, 1901, she was married to Mr. J. H. Koffman, one of Gibson County's most prominent and influential men. Mrs. Koffman is still very much interested in the educational cause, although she does not expect to con-

MRS. J. H. KOFFMAN.

tinue teaching. She is an active member of the Cumberland Presbyterian Church and always takes a great interest in the work of her church.

Dr. J. N. Koffman.

Dr. J. N. Koffman was born in McNairy County, Tenn., on April 5, 1851, and was the second son of James C. and Abigail H. Koffman. He moved with his parents to Gibson County in 1866. His early life was spent on the farm, but he succeeded in acquiring a practical common school education. He took a course at Jones' Commercial College, St. Louis, Mo., and kept books for two years; then he taught school for five years, with considerable success. Dr. Koffman read medicine with Dr. J. W. Penn, of Humboldt, after which he attended the medical department of the University of Nashville and Vanderbilt University, from which institutions he graduated in the spring of 1881. He then entered into the active practice of medicine in which he has since been engaged. He has been a regular and active member of the Gibson County Medical Society since its first organization, and has always stood for the practice of regular medicine, in its various branches. Though busy, he has always stopped to administer to the destitute, sick, and helpless. In 1883 he was married to Miss Mattie E. Motley. This happy union has been blessed with three girls and seven boys, five of whom are living.

Dr. Koffman united with the Baptist Church in the fall of 1870, and participated in the organization of Center Church in 1874, and has served it as clerk for more than twenty years. He has always been a lover of Sunday schools and children who attend Sunday schools, and belongs to that class of citizens who believe in progressive thought. His spare time from the sick room has been employed in growing berries and

fifteen cents per day and board, for Gray Barker, near Old Gibson Church, in the Twentieth District. He worked for some time for Barker and other farmers, and then hired to work at McDowell's mill on middle fork of Forked Deer River.

At about the age of eighteen he married Miss Martha Motley and began housekeeping near the mill; he continued his connection with the mill until after the war, running it

RESIDENCE OF DR. J. N. KOFFMAN, TWENTIETH DISTRICT.

encouraging others to grow them. He has labored hard to build up these favored farm interests in and around Fruitland. His love for country and outdoor life help to make his pleasant humor and good health. The writer always found Dr. Koffman and his noble wife ready to entertain and welcome everyone to their hospitable home.

Austin Bailey and George W. Bailey.

Austin Bailey was born in Wake County, near Raleigh, N. C., on February 14, 1822. He ran away from his father in North Carolina at the age of fourteen, making his way on foot, and in such other ways as he could travel, to Gibson County, Tenn. This was about 1826. He went to work on a farm at

during the war. He owned one-fourth interest in the mill during this time but sold out in anticipation of water power's being superseded by steam. Up to the close of the war, or when the slaves were freed, Mr. Bailey had, by industry, economy, and good management, a sum aggregating $10,000. This he had principally invested in slaves. When the slaves were freed his property and savings were all swept away, leaving him about 150 acres of land. He then devoted himself to farming and had a most excellent helper in his son George, who was born April 11, 1849; and at the close of the war, about the time that Mr. Bailey was passing through the crisis of its disaster, he was able to take a very active part in his father's business. He grad-nally developed such talent for business and work that a great many of the transactions in which his father engaged were entrusted to his hands. He finally became a full partner in all the business. The firm of Bailey & Son is at this time one of the leading firms of the county in farming and real estate operations. Mr. Bailey's rule in life has been to pay as he goes. He never contracts a debt, even in the smallest matters; never goes security for anyone or goes on bond, and of course never asks anyone to go security for him.

Mr. Austin Bailey is now seventy-nine years old, and for many years past has relied on his son George for the active part of his

AUSTIN BAILEY
(Prominent cotton planter and land owner of Gibson County).

business affairs, and for carrying on correspondence and attending to the details of the firm's varied interests.

The firm of Bailey & Son is interested in both the Merchants' State Bank and the Bank of Humboldt, Mr. George W. Bailey being vice president of the Bank of Humboldt.

The firm owns a large amount of farm lands in Gibson and Crockett Counties, amounting to 3,000 acres or more, and business property in Trenton and Humboldt. Mr. George W. Bailey has never married—not on account of any aversion to the female sex, but he says that he has been too busy all his life to look around for a wife, but will have a little leisure from this on, and will give the subject some attention.

Mr. Austin Bailey, though advanced in age, is still active and zealous in business affairs. He is well preserved both in body and mind, and is socially inclined, being fond of the society of young people.

GEORGE W. BAILEY
(Of Bailey & Son, Vice President of Bank of Humboldt).

His religious views correspond to those of the Missionary Baptists. He has always been a very temperate man, has never used tobacco in any form, and eschews liquors of all kinds.

The tax schedule of Gibson County shows the holdings of Bailey & Son to be among the largest in the county. Their taxes—State, county, and municipal—foot up over $700 per annum. Mr. Bailey has a very comfortable home on one of his farms about eight miles west of Humboldt, ten miles southwest of Trenton, and two miles east of Gibson Wells on the Humboldt and Gibson Wells road.

John B. Mitchell, Prominent Farmer.

Mr. John B. Mitchell is one of the progressive and prosperous farmers of the Fruitland neighborhood. He has a beautiful home and a fine farm of 400 acres about three and one-half miles west of Fruitland. He is a native of the Twentieth District, in which he lives, and has been a farmer all his life, and a successful one. He married Miss Sudie Bennett, daughter of Major Bennett, a prominent citizen of Fruitland. They have three promising boys, all little farmers and workers.

Mr. Mitchell is a good, reliable citizen; a member of the Baptist Church at Center, a leading church in the neighborhood. Mr. Mitchell, in addition to operating his large farm, also operates the only self-feeding steam wheat thresher in Gibson County.

Business Enterprises of Fruitland.

J. H. Koffman & Co., general merchants.

H. A. Deming, general merchant.

Mrs. L. D. Brannan, general store.

H. C. Bennett, blacksmith.

R. K. Bennett, Saw and grist mill and cotton gin.

MILAN.

The town of Milan is situated in the southeastern portion of Gibson County, at the crossing of the Jackson Division of the Illinois Central and the Memphis Division of the Louisville and Nashville Railroads. It was incorporated by the Legislature of 1866. The first mayor was John G. Shepherd, who was a merchant. Nearly all of the frame business houses have been torn away and replaced with substantial brick structures. In 1873 H. P. Miller erected the Southern Pacific Hotel building, which is still standing, is kept in good repair, and is, without exception, the handsomest and most commodious hotel building in Tennessee, in a town of Milan's size. It is now operated by E. M. Brown.

The last census gave Milan a population of a little less than 2,000 inhabitants, and she has taken advantage of that fact to rid herself of saloons under the Act of the Legislature of 1899, providing that towns with a population of not more than 2,000 inhabitants may, by surrendering their charters and reincorporating, have the four-mile law applied to them.

The institution of which Milan may well be proudest is her public school system. For the white school she has a large two-story brick building with five classrooms and two large

RESIDENCE OF JOHN B. MITCHELL, PROMINENT FARMER OF TWENTIETH DISTRICT.

halls; also a two-story frame building which is used as a primary department. These two buildings are situated on a beautiful campus of about five acres. The average attendance is about 300 pupils. Eight teachers are employed. The colored school building is a substantial two-room frame structure, situated upon a large and shady campus. The average attendance is fifty, and two teachers are employed. An extra tax of thirty cents on the one hundred dollars' worth of property is levied, and goes exclusively to the support of the schools; besides this the city poll tax and 40 per cent of the privilege and ad valorem taxes goes to the school fund.

In the early part of 1898, at a cost of only about $18,000, Milan completed a splendid water and light plant. The supply of water is afforded by two wells about 175 feet deep. The wells have been tested and the supply has proved inexhaustible. The water is pure and good. The town is well lighted by arc lamps. For the purpose of putting in the plant the town issued $16,000 of bonds. The plant is being economically managed and is beginning to prove a paying investment to the town.

There are seven church organizations in the town and six church buildings. The organizations are Methodist, Baptist, Cumberland, Presbyterian, Christian, Church of Christ, and Christian Scientists. With the exception of the Scientists, all of these own their own buildings.

In the way of manufactories Milan has one roller mill of 120 barrels capacity, one sawmill, one stave factory, one shook factory, and one pea huller factory. The railroad facilities are good and this is a splendid place for a woolen mill and a cotton or knitting mill. An ice factory would pay good dividends at this place.

The city government is composed of a Mayor, Marshal, and six Aldermen. The city officers are as follows: Sid R. Clark, Mayor. Aldermen: C. A. Lacy, S. B. Karnes, R. L. Coley, C. P. Haun, W. C. Barham, and W. T. Dickey. City Marshal, M. S. Clark. Board of Education: E. W. Stone, President; J. R. Harrison, Secretary; R. A. Clopton, B. D. Caldwell, G. W. Williamson, and B. D. Mills.

The history of Milan dates from about 1869, when the Louisville and Nashville Railroad was built through the county. The railroad established a depot at this point and called it Milan. The United States postal authorities established a postoffice at the same time.

After the Civil War the town grew considerably, and in 1872, when the Illinois Central Railroad built its line through the county, crossing the Louisville and Nashville here, the town became a place of importance. It had a population in 1880 of 1,200 and did an extensive business; in 1890 the population was 1,546; in 1900 it was 1,682.

B. A. Williamson was the first railroad agent and postmaster at Milan.

The Churches of Milan.

The Baptist Church was organized in 1867. Some of the first members of the church who participated in the organization at that time were S. P. Clark and wife; R. H. Clark; R. B. Hutchinson and wife; E. A. Collins and wife; Rev. James M. Hurst and wife and daughter; Zach Jackson, Dr. Arthur Pearce, and others, in all about fifteen. The first pastor was the Rev. James M. Hurst. The congregation worshiped in the old Masonic Hall until 1870, when the present brick church building was erected. Only three members of the original congregation are now living— E. A. Collins and wife, and R. A. Clark. The present membership of the church is 234; of the Sunday school, 100. The present pastor is the Rev. W. H. Sledge, who has been in charge of the church since 1898.

The Congregation of the Methodist Episcopal Church, South, was organized about 1865, and worshiped, prior to the erection of the present church building, in the old Masonic Hall, since torn down. The present church building was erected in 1868. The first pastor was O. P. Parker, in 1868. Since then the following have served the church as pastor: J. H. Garrett, W. T. Bowling, Ed Organ, T. L. Sanders, J. E. Beck, W. H. Leigh, B. F. Peeples, J. M. Scott, A. L. Pritchett, J. M. Maxwell, M. M. Taylor, W. H. Armstrong, R. M. King, E. B. Graham, B. A. Hays, W. T. Lock, J. T. Wiggins, B. F. Blackman, W. W. Adams, W. D. Jenkins, and S. B. Love. The present pastor is J. R. Hardin. The present membership of the church is 243, and of the Snday school, 250. The auxiliary societies are: The Woman's Missionary, Juvenile Missionary, Home Parsonage Society, and Epworth League, all of which are well sustained. In 1900 revival services in the church resulted in 102 conversions and an addition to the church of fifty members.

The Christian Church was organized in 1897. W. T. Bowles was its first pastor. At present the church has no regular pastor. The congregation holds services every Sunday. Occasionally Elder E. C. L. Denton and others preach for them. Mr. Denton's home is in Milan. He preaches for several churches in Henry and Carroll Counties, Tenn., and Calloway County, Ky.

The Cumberland Presbyterian Church is one of the oldest in Milan. It is a very prosperous church with 150 members.

Church of Christ (Scientists).

This is an organized body of worshipers having readings and services every Sunday at the rooms of the society at D. A. Taylor's residence. The society was organized in 1893. The organizers and prominent members are Mrs. Minor P. Moore, Mrs. E. N. Stone, and Mrs. D. A. Taylor.

W. H. Coley.

Mr. W. H. Coley, of Milan, Tenn., is the proprietor of the Coley Drug Co., of Milan; director in the Milan Banking Co.; vice president of the True-Tagg Paint Co., of Memphis, Tenn., and a director in the Puryear-Miller Manufacturing Co. and the VanVleet-Mansfield Drug Co., of Memphis, Tenn.

Mr. Coley is a native of Gibson County, and has made his home in the county all his life. His connection with the various important business enterprises mentioned sufficiently indicate his business ability and activity. He is well known throughout West Tennessee, having for some eighteen years represented the VanVleet-Mansfield Drug Company in that section of the State.

In his home community Mr. Coley occupies a high social position, and is especially helpful and ready in all measures and movements promotive of the public good.

RESIDENCE OF W. H. COLEY, MILAN, TENN.

W. C. Barham.

Mr. Barham's home and business headquarters are at Milan. He operates a stock farm near Milan, devoting his farm operations to the breeding of shorthorn cattle and registered horses, also grazing stock. He is the owner of some of the best bred saddle stallions in the State, namely: King Duluth, No. 20, S. H. R.; Brown Squirrel, No. 1114; Tennessee Denmark, No. 1239; and others equally as well bred. More mares are bred to his horses than to any others in the county. He transacts an extensive general shipping business in live stock, his transactions covering an aggregate of $50,000 per annum in this line alone.

He has shipped since August, 1900, $40,000 worth of stock, embracing horses, cattle, and hogs.

Mr. Barham was born in Carroll County, near the line of Gibson, in 1858, of North Carolina parentage and has followed the business of farming, stock raising, and breeding, all his life.

He has made his home in Milan since December, 1897. He is a member of the Board of Aldermen of the city of Milan and is active in the promotion of the well-being and progress of his town and county. He is a member of the Methodist Episcopal Church, Woodmen of the World, and Ancient Order of United Workmen, in all of which relations he is a liberal and helpful worker.

In 1882 he married Miss Maggie Manning, an estimable young lady and a member of a prominent family of Gibson County, a sister of P. H. Manning, of Montgomery Bell Academy and Peabody Normal College, of Nashville, one of the leading educators of the State. Mr. and Mrs. Barham have three

W. C. BARHAM
(Prominent stockman and stock dealer of Gibson County).

children, two sons and a daughter, to bless their union, all of whom are bright and promising children.

People's Bank of Milan.

Incorporated under the general laws of the State in 1889; authorized capital, $40,000. D. A. Taylor, President; D. A. Belew, Vice President; J. R. Harrison, Cashier; W. E. McNail, Assistant Cashier. Directors: D. A. Taylor, D. C. Caldwell, B. A. Denney, J. R. Harrison, D. A. Belew, D. H. Wyont, J. L. Culp, W. R. Smith, John D. Denney, B. F. Johnson, B. D. Mills.

Milan Banking Company.

Incorporated under the general laws of the State in 1893. Authorized capital, $50,000; $25,000 paid in. President, B. A. Denney; vice president, M. W. Wheeler; cashier, Fred Collins; assistant cashier, L. P. Dodson. Directors: M. W. Wheeler, D. H. Wyont. J. L. Culp, J. P. Rhodes, W. J. Rust, D. A. Taylor, E. A. Collins, J. C. Cheek, W. H. Coley, John Roper, L. P. Dodson, A. R. Dodson, B. A. Denney, Jeff J. Blanks, Fred Collins.

Dr. Robert A. Clopton.

Dr. Robert A. Clopton is a graduate of the Eclectic Medical Institute, Cincinnati, O., Class of 1878. He is local surgeon of the Louisville and Nashville Railroad, a member of the National Eclectic Medical Association, of the Tennessee State Eclectic Medical Society, and of the Medical Society of the State of Tennessee. He makes a specialty of gynecology and electro-therapeutics, and bears the reputation of a first-class practitioner.

Dr. Clopton has lived at Milan for sixteen years, having during that time demonstrated his ability as a physician and surgeon in the cure of diseases and the treatment of surgical cases.

A remarkable feature of Dr. Clopton's method of treatment of diseases is the electrical apparatus with which his room is equipped. The static electric and X-ray machine used by the Doctor in his practice is one of the most powerful in the State of Tennessee, which, together with other modern and up-to-date appliances, such as hot air apparatus, surgical devices and instruments,

DR. ROBERT A. CLOPTON.
(Noted physician and surgeon of Milan).

costing large sums of money, would do honor to a first-class infirmary or sanitarium.

The Doctor is one of Milan's best citizens, progressive in his ideas and helpful in all movements for his town and county. He is a firm believer in prohibition and votes for the abolition of the whisky traffic.

The Press of Milan.

THE MILAN EXCHANGE.

The Milan Exchange was established by W. A. Wade in 1874. Mr. Wade was a well-known newspaper man of Tennessee, having conducted the Lebanon Democrat, at Lebanon, Tenn., before coming to Gibson County.

The Exchange has been one of the leading newspapers of Gibson County since its establishment. It is the oldest newspaper in the county. The paper is still owned by the widow of Mr. Wade, Mrs. Cora M. Wade.

The editorial and business management of the Exchange is conducted by Mr. George Williamson, a nephew of Mr. Wade, and a young man of excellent literary and business ability, who is making it an influential factor in the affairs of Milan and the county of Gibson.

THE MILAN HUSTLER

was established on November 11, 1893, with James Holt, Jr., and Frank Chambers as editors. In August, 1894, Beverly Williamson purchased Mr. Chambers' interest, and in 1895 he purchased Mr. Holt's interest, and since that time has been editor and owner of the paper.

The Hustler is a five-column quarto, four pages home print. It has always been a supporter of Democracy and Democratic principles.

Milan Business Directory.

Agricultural Implements and Hardware.—York & McCracken, C. A. Lacy, T. L. Harmon Hardware Company.

Banks.—People's, Milan Banking Company.

Bakeries.—E. Keiliber.

Barbers.—Taylor & Co., Ed Childress, Jesse Shankle.

Blacksmiths.—W. Dickey.

Dry Goods.—Milan Dry Goods Company, G. W. Wilson, Lacy & Kearns, R. J. Burrow, W. A. Wilson, W. B. William & Son, Threadgill & Co., A. Chambers.

Dentists.—H. K. Fink.

Drugs.—Coley Drug Company, A. M. Bingham.

Furniture.—Bodkin Brothers, York & McCracken, C. A. Lacy.

Groceries.—W. P. Williams, M. W. Wheeler, J. R. Persons, Oliver & Wilson, C. A. Lacy, Carter & McCoy, W. J. Rust, Peeler & Hammond, Wallace Harlan.

Hotels.—Commercial, Southern Pacific, Woods Home.

Insurance.—Sid R. Clark, E. N. Stone, J. P. Rhodes, J. R. Harrison.

Jewelers.—Charles Howe.

Lawyers.—J. P. Rhodes, Sid R. Clark, H. M. Clark, Ed Smith.

Liverymen.—W. D. Kizer, W. C. Barham, Black & Oakley.

Laundries.—Milan Steam.

Milliners.—Miss Bessie Allington, Mrs. Clint Mathis.

Meat Markets.—E. L. Butler.

Newspapers.—Milan Hustler, Milan Exchange.

Physicians.—R. A. Clopton, A. E. Cox, B. D. Caldwell, L. G. Danner.

Produce, Feed, and Grain.—Pittman & Williams, W. C. Barham, T. C. Mathis.

Restaurants.—Wallace Harlan, Martha Richardson, colored.

Saddlery.—W. C. Barham, York & McCracken.

Shoes.—Charles Kastner.

Shoemakers.—Alf Doak.

Undertakers.—York & McCracken, Bodkin Brothers.

Manufacturing Plants.—Todd & Roper, shooks and staves; Milan Pea Thresher Manufacturing Company; W. L. Patrick, lumber; W. J. & J. A. Keaton, McDonald & Co., staves; Milan Milling Company.

POST OFFICES IN GIBSON COUNTY.

There are thirty-four post offices in the county, as follows: Trenton, Humboldt, Milan, Dyer, Rutherford, Fruitland, Cedar, Gibson, West, Hollyleaf, Gann, Cades, Idlewild, Bradford, Skullbone, Clareville, Edmunds, Laneview, Knightville, Newell, Tyson, Yorkville, Neboville, Hooten, Fairview, Eaton, Brazil, Lex, Gibson Wells, Ava, Grizzard, Medina, Lonoke, and Currie.

BRAZIL.

The village of Brazil is situated in the Fifth Civil District, about nine miles southwest of Trenton. The place was settled about 1867 or 1868. W. W. Simmons and W. S. Hartsfield established a general store here at that time, which induced others to establish themselves in different branches of trade and business, and the place gradually became a considerable center of trade.

The country around Brazil is well adapted to general farming, some of the land being

METHODIST CHURCH, BRAZIL.

very productive. The farmers in the neighborhood cultivate a variety of crops, and are generally prosperous. There are two churches in the town, Methodist and Presbyterian. The Methodist people have a very handsome new frame church, and the Presbyterians are preparing to build a new house of worship. There are no resident pastors in the village. Rev. W. J. Naylor, of Trenton, preaches one Sunday and night each month for the Methodists, and Rev. R. I. Long preaches once a month for the Presbyterians. Both congregations are prosperous and growing. The Methodist Church has a membership of fifty-seven and a Sunday school of eighty-five pupils. Dr. W. F. Mathews is superintendent of the Sunday school. The Presbyterians number about sixty.

The Methodists have a strong church at Bower's Chapel, two miles west of Brazil. This church has 125 members, served by W. J. Naylor once a month.

The school at Brazil is graded, and has an enrollment of 240 pupils. Under the management of Prof. E. L. Boone it has acquired a good reputation for efficiency.

Some of the oldest residents of Brazil are: W. B. Howse, B. M. Dodd, and W. S. Hartsfield.

The firm of Howse & Ragan, composed of W. W. Howse and Bennett Ragan, operates the largest mercantile business in Brazil. This firm carries a stock of general merchandise aggregating $10,000 in value. They have a large trade.

Other firms, all of whom do more or less business, are: Ragan & Banks, Mrs. G. W. Dabney (general stores).

Parkinson & Brassfield operate a steam roller mill of forty-barrel capacity. This firm also operates a sawmill and cotton gin.

Albert Adcock and Harrison & Lane are general blacksmiths and repairers.

The physicians of Brazil are: Dr. Albert Brassfield and Dr. W. F. Mathews.

Joe R. Thompson.

Joe R. Thompson is a native of Rutherford County, Tenn., and was born on a farm in 1851. When quite young he moved with his father's family to Gibson County, Tenn., in which county he has since resided, most of the time on a farm near the little town of Brazil. He has a classical education, and is well read in history, politics, and literature. He was educated for a lawyer, and has license to practice in all the courts of the State; but for reasons satisfactory to himself he has never engaged in the active practice of his profession, being content to remain a practical farmer, as he was raised.

He is a member of the Methodist Church, and is a strong advocate of, and active worker

FRONT VIEW OF HOWSE & RAGAN'S GENERAL STORE.

in, the Sunday school. In politics he is a Democrat, and has done his party and his friends good service. He has never sought office, though often solicited by his friends to do so, rather desiring to remain in the ranks and work for his friends. He may yet, however, be heard from on the hustings and in the arena of public affairs.

He has the elements of an orator; and had he entered the active practice of the law and into the political field, he would have risen, no doubt, to distinction.

At present and for several years he has been an acting justice of the peace for the Fifth Civil District of his county; and as a member of the County Court he stands well to the front, taking an active and leading part in public questions, and representing his district and people on the floor of the court with credit and honor.

Dr. W. F. Mathews.

Dr. Mathews is a native Tennessean, having been born in Williamson County, near Franklin, on January 11, 1855. He was brought up on a farm, and received his pri-

JOE R. THOMPSON
(Member of County Court from Fifth District).

RESIDENCE OF DR. ALBERT BRASSFIELD.

mary education in the common schools and an academic education at Hardeman Academy. He studied medicine, and graduated at Vanderbilt University in 1880, and entered active practice at McKenzie, Tenn., the same year. He practiced six years at that point, and then removed to Brazil, his present home, in 1886.

In 1887 he married Miss Fannie B. Howse, daughter of one of the pioneer and prominent families of Gibson County.

The Doctor has built up a large practice in the neighborhood of his home, and so far as the material things of life are concerned, he has been eminently prosperous.

He has a pleasant home and pleasant home surroundings and happy domestic relations. He has two promising boys, Edward C. and Lonnie F., now attending school and preparing for useful men.

The Doctor and his wife are prominent members of the Methodist Episcopal Church, South, at Brazil, and the Doctor is superintendent of the Sunday school, which is in a most prosperous condition under his management and supervision. He and his family stand high in the social world, and have the universal respect and esteem of the entire community.

YORKVILLE AND ITS NEIGHBORHOOD.

This flourishing village is situated in the Eighth Civil District of the county, about ten miles west of Dyer. It is one of the oldest-settled places in the county, and its neighborhood witnessed the first permanent church organizations in the county. The Cumberland Presbyterians had an organization here as far back as 1825. The Baptists and Methodists also were early in this field with church organizations.

The village itself was probably located about 1826. It is a sort of tradition that the first settler and founder of Yorkville was a man named Kuykendall, who set up a store which proved the nucleus of a town. At any rate, the town of to-day is quite a business and social center, and is surrounded by a most excellent farming country and community.

It has two churches and a well-conducted

DR. W. F. MATHEWS AND FAMILY.

free school, with an enrollment of 185 pupils. Camp meetings were held for many years by the Cumberland Presbyterians on the site of the town, and the present Cumberland Presbyterian Church stands on a portion of the old camp ground. Many of the older inhabitants of the Yorkville neighborhood remember the stirring scenes of old camp-meeting times. The last camp meeting was held about 1850.

The Yorkville neighborhood is distinguished for the sobriety and moral tone of its people. There is no saloon in the town or neighborhood.

General variety stores are conducted by the following firms: H. E. Wilson, J. A. Wherry, F. M. Pipkin, and L. N. Pipkin; Claud Bone, dealer in drugs and medicines; Alvin Dolin and S. M. Pipkin, groceries; Inman Brothers, hardware and farm implements. Inman Brothers also operate a sawmill and planing mill and cotton gin. May & Hammond are blacksmiths and woodworkers.

In and around Yorkville there are six flourishing churches. In Yorkville are the Cumberland Presbyterian and Christian Churches. One mile south is Bethel Baptist Church. Nebo (Methodist) is three and one-half miles south; Hopewell (Methodist) is two and one-half miles east; and four miles in the same direction is Bell's Chapel, a Cumberland Presbyterian Church. The same denomination has another church one and one-half miles north.

The farming interests of the section are well advanced. The lands are productive, and, for the most part, the farmers are prosperous. Without disparagement to others, I mention a number of gentlemen I met who are prominent as farmers and many of whom are old citizens of the community: R. G. Scott, J. K. P. Hale, T. J. Cooper, D. A. Ramsey; W. H., J. T., and S. A. Bradley; J. D., R. L., and S. J. Overall; A. H. Sandford, H. Banks, N. B. Walters, E. C. Womble, G. B. and L. T. Holland, J. W. Pierce, W. F. Pierce, J. A. Skipper, W. T. Davis, R. F. Pique, J. C. and J. T. Carlton, Howard Huie, S. B. and L. M. Logan, and Joe S. McCorkle.

The principal crops raised in the Eighth District are wheat and corn. But little cotton is produced. Vegetables and grasses are cultivated to a considerable extent. A good deal of attention is paid to stock raising, and there is a good annual product of horses, mules, cattle, and hogs. In a word, it may be said of the Eighth District generally that it is well up in agricultural progress.

H. L. Wyatt.

H. L. Wyatt, one of the magistrates of the Eighth District, has been a resident of the village of Yorkville since 1858. His long residence in the community and the interest he has taken in public affairs has given him prominence in the community. In addition to his duties as magistrate, he officiates as a notary public. He also carries on successfully the farming business. Mr. Wyatt is a

H. L. WYATT
(A prominent citizen of Yorkville and member of the County Court).

leading member of the Cumberland Presbyterian Church, and is a zealous promoter of the religious and educational interests of his town and neighborhood. He is a man of upright character and sober habits. He is a strong advocate of the cause of temperance, and practices what he preaches, never having used intoxicants or tobacco in his life.

RUTHERFORD.

The town of Rutherford, in the Ninth District, was located in about 1857. The contiguous farming section in the Eighth, Ninth, Tenth, Eleventh, Nineteenth, and Twenty-first Districts, consisting of fine producing land, has made it a place of considerable trade. The town was incorporated in about 1866.

Two years ago the town got rid of its saloon incubus, and is now one of the most orderly places in the county. There are three good churches, with prosperous congregations and Sabbath schools. They are the Methodists, Baptists, and Cumberland Presbyterians. There are also three colored churches of the same denominations.

The town has a good school, in which the

statutory branches are taught, with two additional grades. H. H. Ellis is the principal of the school, with Mrs. Ellis and Miss Threlkeld as assistants. Miss Jessie Bittick is the music teacher. Miss Gentry Ward is assistant in the primary department. The school enrollment is 235.

The town government is as follows:
Mayor, A. H. Taylor.
Recorder, Wright McDaniel.
Marshal, W. H. Worrel.
Aldermen: P. H. Northan, W. T. H. Thorne, M. Peel, G. M. Savage, and J. E. Kyzer.

Rutherford Business Directory.

Physicians.—J. B. Rickman, J. W. Allen, J. W. Daniel.

General Stores, Dry Goods, etc.—Northan & McDaniel, M. Peel, F. W. E. Flowers, and Haguewood, Kennedy & Elrod.

Groceries, Hardware, and Saddlery.—Davidson & Conlee.

Groceries.—Courtney & Glisson, Arnold & Thomas, J. C. Holmes.

Confectioneries.—Savage & Stubblefield.

Drugs.—M. A. Terry, R. E. Armstrong, R. B. Tinkle.

Hotels.—Commercial Hotel.

Banks.—The Bank of Rutherford.

Roller Mills.—The Rutherford Milling Company.

Planing Mills.—Davidson & Conlee.

Blacksmiths and Woodworkers.—N. L. Davis.

The Masons have a lodge, of which J. W. C. Fain is Worshipful Master and W. P. McCullum is Secretary.

Leonidas Lodge, Knights of Pythias, with a membership of forty, is located here.

The Odd Fellows (Rutherford Lodge, No. 120), with a membership of twenty, is located in Rutherford.

J. W. Boyett operates a store and farm about seven miles out from Rutherford, at Tyson Post Office, in the Twenty-fourth District. F. B. Boyett is postmaster at this point.

The Bank of Rutherford

was organized in 1898 under the general laws of the State. The following are its officers: W. P. Elrod, president; J. E. Kyzer, vice president; Luther Porter, cashier.

Rutherford Milling Company,

organized in February, 1900, is an extensive manufacturing establishment, with a capacity of 100 barrels of flour per day. H. C. Hopper, president; A. H. Taylor, vice president; W. D. Hopper, secretary.

J. E. Kyzer.

Mr. Kyzer is a native of South Carolina. He came to Gibson County in January, 1859, and began business in general merchandising at Rutherford, at that time a new station on the Mobile and Ohio Railroad. The road had just been completed, and its first through passenger trains were run through the county in the spring of 1859. Mr. Kyzer continued in the general merchandise business until 1900, a period of over forty years, during that time accumulating a competency. Although industrious, frugal, and devoted to business, he never was grasping in disposition, but conducted his life and business on the live-and-let-live principle. In consequence he bears the reputation among his neighbors and in the community as a truly upright man. No better compliment could be paid him than that he is universally respected by all. He is a member of the Cumberland Presbyterian Church, of Rutherford, and is helpful in all his church relations. He is a member of the Town Council, vice president and a director in the Bank of Rutherford, the only bank in the town. Since retiring from active business he devotes his attention to the management of his farms in the neighborhood of Rutherford. His home in Rutherford is a model of convenience and comfort, and his domestic relations are of the happiest character.

NEBOVILLE AND NEIGHBORHOOD.

This little village, in the Eighth District, is the seat of a splendid school, known as the Neboville High School. This school has more than a local reputation as an educational institution. In addition to the prescribed State curriculum, the full course of study embraces the higher branches of learning, so that pupils are given the benefit of a thorough academic course. The very best instructors are provided, and the school is fully equipped and systematized for imparting an education. Boarding pupils are provided for, so that an education may be obtained at the institution at very moderate cost. The school is under the management of a board of education.

He has a beautiful home, furnished with every modern convenience obtainable in a country location. It was my good fortune to partake of the Doctor's hospitality during my visit to the Eighth District. I found him to be a man energetic and pushing in business and professional affairs, but not unmindful of the graces of social life.

RESIDENCE OF DR. A. E. TURNER
(A noted physician of near Neboville, and member of the State Senate from Gibson County).

This board is composed of the following gentlemen: Dr. A. E. Turner, secretary; A. H. Sandford, J. T. Carlton, H. Banks, N. C. Corley, R. Q. Scott, J. A. Skipper, and J. C. Carlton. The first three of these are the school directors of the district, who act in conjunction with the others in the control of the Neboville High School.

The village of Neboville is pleasantly situated in a well-improved farming country and well fitted as a location for a school. There are two general stores in the village, conducted by J. N. Tidrow and J. A. Teague & Co.

Dr. A. E. Turner, whose portrait appears on another page in connection with the county officials (being State Senator), resides in the neighborhood. Dr. Turner, in addition to his practice as a physician, carries on a large grain and stock farm, which he manages most successfully, breeding and raising Durham and Jersey cattle and thoroughbred horses.

KENTON

is situated on the Mobile and Ohio Railroad, 60 miles south of Cairo, Ill., and 215 miles from St. Louis, Mo. The town is located partly in Gibson County and partly in Obion County. The population of Kenton is 670, according to the census returns of 1900. The principal residence portion of the town is in Gibson County, while, on account of the railroad, the business portion is mostly in Obion County.

All the churches of the town are in Gibson County. The religious denominations are: Methodist, Cumberland Presbyterian, Baptist, and Christian. The Methodists have a very good brick church; the other churches have comfortable frame buildings.

The Methodists have a membership of 140, with Rev. Wilber Mooney as pastor. Its Sunday school has 110 pupils; J. L. Fry, superintendent. The Cumberland Presbyterian Church has a membership of 150, with

Rev. J. L. Dickens as pastor. Its Sunday school has 115 pupils; C. G. Tilghman, superintendent. The Baptist Church has a membership of 130, with Rev. J. W. Early as pastor. The Christian congregation has a membership of 20.

The Kenton Academy building is a large, handsome brick structure, built in 1895 on the ground upon which stood a former building, burned in 1895. A nine-months free school is maintained, with an enrollment of 200 pupils. Prof. C. A. Derryberry has charge of the school as principal, with Mrs. Belle Jones, Mrs. Susie Nooner, and Miss Jettye Page as assistants. There are ten grades taught.

The history of the town dates from the completion of the Mobile and Ohio Railroad, in 1858. The first business conducted in the place was that of a general store by C. S. Hooper & Co. But little business was done until after the war. At the present time a considerable trade is carried on in agricultural products and farm supplies.

The country about Kenton consists of fine farming lands, and the farmers are an industrious and prosperous class.

The town was first incorporated in 1874. The present corporate officers are:

Mayor, R. H. McNeely.
Recorder, W. A. Montgomery.
Aldermen: Dr. E. A. Taylor, J. N. Tull, C. R. Wade, W. H. Wilson (also Treasurer), John D. Carroll, J. A. Reeves.
Marshal, W. R. White.
School Board (Gibson County): J. W. Howell, secretary; T. M. Bogle, J. R. Carroll.
School Board (Obion County): E. P. Buchanan, chairman; J. N. Tull, J. D. Carroll.

Business Establishments of Kenton.

The town of Kenton has a very large trade in both Gibson and Obion Counties, and its business establishments are important, carrying large stocks and doing an extensive business.

Agricultural Implements and Machinery.—Clarence Bogle, C. R. Wade.

Banks.—Kenton Bank, organized in 1892; authorized capital, $50,000; paid in, $30,000. President, G. P. Hurt; vice president, W. F. Collins; cashier, Walter Howell. Directors: C. R. Wade, T. M. Bogle, W. A. White, M. E. Watts, W. F. Collins, and G. W. Reed. People's Bank, organized in 1901; capital paid, $20,000. President, John R. Carroll; vice president, Henry Flowers; cashier, G. W. Reed; assistant cashier, Hal J. Ramer. Directors: R. C. Tilghman, Dr. E. A. Taylor, Sol Shatz, J. B. Layne, Henry Flowers, and G. W. Reed.

RESIDENCE OF C. R. WADE, ONE OF THE LEADING MERCHANTS OF KENTON.

Barbers.—J. F. Eddelman.
Blacksmiths.—A. Warts, T. W. Hall.
Carpenters and Builders.—H. Seever, Frank Summers, J. A. Harrison.
Cotton Gins.—Wade & Wade.
Dry Goods.—D. A. Pate, Kenton Stock Company, Gentry Reynolds, T. W. Jones, Shatz & Co., Watkins & Wade, J. L. Bingham.
Dentists.—L. E. Taylor, C. C. Powell.

Drug Stores.—Montgomery & Bogle, C. A. Hudson, Taylor & Turner.

Furniture and Undertakers.—C. R. Wade.

Flouring Mills.—Reliance Milling Company.

Grain and Produce.—Bogle & Tull, T. M. Bogle, Reliance Milling Company.

Groceries.—D. J. Keathley, M. L. Corley, Taylor & Turner, Reeves & Wade.

Hotels.—Commercial, Lindel.

Hardware.—C. R. Wade, Clarence Bogle.

Insurance.—J. W. Howell, G. W. Reed.

Jewelers.—D. F. Barnwell.

Lawyers.—J. L. Fry, E. R. Bruce.

Liverymen.—J. W. Patterson.

Milliners.—Watkins & Wade, J. L. Bingham.

Meat Markets.—A. Worts.

Physicians.—H. T. Fullerton, F. J. Ramer, S. N. Page, G. J. Ramsey, A. J. Skiles, A. J. Taylor, E. A. Taylor.

Public Halls.—Central Hall (for lectures and public meetings); seating capacity, 500.

Shoemakers.—N. P. Eddelman.

Stave Mills.—W. B. Shannon.

Temperance Drinks.—J. F. Carroll.

John W. Howell.

John W. Howell, justice of the peace and notary public, Kenton, Tenn., was born in Gibson County, Tenn., on September 10, 1841. He is a son of Jethro and grandson of Caleb Howell, a North Carolinian, who came with his family to Gibson County in 1825, and settled four miles southwest of Kenton. Jethro Howell was born in North Carolina on November 7, 1818, and died on October 23, 1894. He married Elizabeth Needham in 1840, who was a daughter of Rev. John W. Needham, who came to Gibson County from Maryland about 1822, and was the first sheriff of Gibson County and a minister in the Cumberland Presbyterian Church. Mr. Howell is of Scotch-Irish descent, and was reared on a farm and educated in the country schools. From 1858 to 1861 he traded in stock, shipping to New Orleans, and in the year 1861 he enlisted in the Confederate Army at Columbus, Ky., in Company H, Thirteenth Tennessee Infantry; but on account of disabilities he was discharged the same year. In the year 1863 he reënlisted in the Twelfth Tennesseee Cavalry under General Forrest, and was afterwards transferred to the Second Tennessee Cavalry, serving until the close of the war, in May, 1865, receiving a parole at Paducah, Ky. He came to Kenton in the fall of 1869, where he has

JOHN W. HOWELL
(Member of County Court).

since, until 1900, been engaged in mercantile pursuits.

Mr. Howell is a Democrat in politics, and was elected justice of the peace in 1876, and reëlected in 1882, serving twelve years; and being opposed to a third term, he was not a candidate in 1888. In 1894 his friends again elected him justice of the peace, and reëlected him in 1900; and in 1899, when Gibson County Court found it necessary to build a new courthouse, he, with R. Z. Taylor, Dr. T. J. Happel, John P. Hale, and B. C. Jarrell, was put on the Building Committee, the result of whose labors is that one of the best, if not the very best, courthouses in the State has been completed.

He was married in September, 1862, to Amanda C. Dozier, who was born in Gibson County on January 2, 1846.

Mr. Howell is a Mason, Odd Fellow, and a Knight of Pythias. He was made a Mason in March and Knight Templar in December, 1863, and has been Recorder of Kenton Commandery, No. 18, Knights Templar, since it was organized in June, 1891. He has filled other positions in the various lodges to which he belonged. He and his wife are members of the Cumberland Presbyterian Church. He was ordained an elder in 1866, and has been stated clerk and treasurer of Obion Presbytery since 1886.

He has lived in Kenton thirty-two years, and there are but two other persons who are older citizens of the town. He is now about sixty years of age, and a leading citizen and a representative man of Gibson County.

Mr. Howell is universally esteemed for his probity of character and good citizenship.

Rev. J. L. Dickens.

Rev. J. L. Dickens, D.D., LL.D., was born in Gibson County, Tenn., and received his primary education in the common schools of the county. When a boy he became a Christian, and joined the Cumberland Presbyterian Church. He became a candidate for the ministry under the care of the Hopewell Presbytery of the Cumberland Presbyterian Church before he was grown, and entered Newberne Academy and studied there two years. He was licensed to preach, and then entered Bethel College, and was a student in said college about five years, from which college he was graduated with the degree of A.B. in June, 1879. He studied theology in Lane Seminary, Cincinnati, O., and Cumberland University, Lebanon, Tenn., and was graduated from the last-named university with the degree of B.D. in 1884. In the same year he was elected to a professorship in Bethel College, McKenzie, Tenn. He completed a post-graduate course in McKendree College, of Lebanon, Ill., and received the A.M. degree in 1885. In 1886 he was chosen president of Bethel College, McKenzie, Tenn. In 1887 he completed a post-graduate course of study in metaphysical and ethical philosophy in Cumberland University and received the Ph.D. degree. He was chosen president of Trinity University, Texas, in 1889. In 1891 he became president of Quanah College, Texas. In this same year Butler University, Indiana, conferred upon him the degree of LL.D. He served Quanah College until the building was destroyed by fire in December, 1893. He returned to Tennessee, and was pastor of the Cumberland Presbyterian Church, Murfreesboro, until he was again chosen president of Bethel College in 1895. Four years again he served as president of this college. In 1899 Florence College, Texas, conferred the degree of D.D. upon him. He became pastor of the Cumberland Presbyterian Church in Kenton in 1899. In May,

REV. J. L. DICKENS
(Pastor of Cumberland Presbyterian Church, Kenton).

1901, the American University, of Harriman, Tenn., conferred the degree of S.T.D. upon him after an advanced post-graduate course in theology.

Mr. Dickens has been married twice—the first time, to Miss Mattie Tiner, of Gibson County, Tenn.; the second time, to Miss Mary Elizabeth Bridforth, of Nesbitt, Miss. The first marriage was shortly after his graduation from Bethel College; the second marriage was on December 25, 1895.

MEDINA.

This is a village of 300 inhabitants, situated in a fine fruit and grain-growing section of the county, on the Illinois Central Railroad, nine miles south of Milan. The business interests of Medina are represented by the following establishments:

Drugs.—D. T. Andrews.

Dry Goods.—Shatz & Cunningham, S. Tuchfield & Sons, H. M. House.

General Merchants.—D. B. Rowlett.
Groceries.—I. M. Nelson, J. C. McDonald, A. M. House, T. J. Graves, J. D. McClutchon, J. A. Mayo.
Furniture and Undertakers.—W. M. Senter.
Hotels.—Andrew House.
Liverymen.—Coburn & Spain, S. Fuzzell.
Blacksmiths.—B. O. Smith.
Roller Mills.—G. R. James & Co.
Undertakers.—McCulley & Turner.
Cotton Gins.—Rowlett Brothers.

DR. D. T. ANDREWS
(Merchant).

Lumber and Timber Dealers.—J. W. Morris.
Box Timber and Fertilizers.—R. M. Hemphill.
Physicians.—J. E. Adkisson, J. D. Richardson, J. A. Blackman.
Dentists.—Cole Gillespie.
Postmaster.—R. N. Karnes.

There are three churches in the town—Methodist, Baptist, and Cumberland Presbyterian—all with flourishing congregations and well-attended Sunday schools.

The town has a good graded free school under State law.

Medina is the shipping point for a considerable territory devoted to fruit and vegetable growing, besides other farm products. A few of the leading fruit growers who ship from this point are: A. Graves, W. O. Graves, J. J. Parish, J. L. Mills, W. W. Roe, J. H. Barnwell, J. H. Jackson & Bro., T. Warmath,

MRS. AGGIE ANDREWS.

John Warmath, H. H. Love, and William Daughterty.

J. C. Shelton is the obliging railroad agent at Medina.

GIBSON STATION

is a station and village on the Louisville and Nashville Railroad, five miles east of Humboldt. It is an important shipping point for fruits, vegetables, and general farm products. There is a fine section of productive farming land adjacent, constituting one of the best neighborhoods in the county. This point ships an aggregate of 230 car loads of garden products per annum to Northern markets.

The village has two handsome frame churches, occupied by the Methodists and Baptists. The Methodists have a membership of 110 and a Sunday school of 75; the Baptists have a membership of 153 and a Sunday school of 100.

A good school is maintained, having an enrollment of 150 pupils.

The business enterprises are:
General Stores.—S. A. Scruggs and W. J. Rust.
Groceries, Drugs, and Hardware.—J. F. Parker.
Groceries.—Meals & Chandler.
Fruit Boxes, Timber, and Fertilizers.—James L. Morgan.
Fertilizers.—H. M. Fly.

Blacksmiths.—E. L. Cannon.
Physicians.—R. H. Hunt, T. D. Bugg, C. S. Parker.

BRADFORD

is a flourishing little town on the Illinois Central Railroad, in the northeastern part of the county, of 350 inhabitants. It is situated in a good farming region and enjoys a good trade. It was located about 1874 on the completion of the railroad through the county.

The town has a good graded free school, with a high school department which has a very high standing in the community.

The Methodists, Baptists, and Cumberland Presbyterians have good church buildings and prosperous congregations.

The business enterprises of the town are:
General Merchants.—Boone, Belew & Co.; J. A. Smith, Meadors & Overton, Alexander Bros. & Green.
Drugs.—J. W. Crider.
Groceries.—T. J. Collins, F. M. Campbell.
Grain Dealers.—J. Candle & Son.
Stock Breeders.—G. T. Belew.
Liverymen.—R. L. Lannom.
Undertakers.—J. W. Johns.
Blacksmiths and Wagon Makers.—J. H. Hedgcock.
Hotels.—N. I. H. McKenzie.
Physicians.—J. D. and J. A. McKenzie and J. A. Moore.

The principal industries in operation are:
Cotton Ginners.—Smith, Arnold & Co.; J. E. Conlee & Co.
Roller Mills.—J. T. Cain & Son.

The agricultural products shipped from this point indicate the productiveness of the farms in the country around: Fruits and vegetables, 145 cars; live stock and poultry, 175 cars; timber products (embracing lumber, sawed and hewn, split timber, staves, and uncut logs), 800 cars.

The following are a few of the largest shippers of farm products: D. L. Patrick, A. Anderson, J. N. Thetford, J. M. Guy, E. V. Guy, J. N. Rochelle, W. H. Desmond, J. K. McAlister, J. M. Ford, and J. R. Moore.

IDLEWILD,

a station on the Illinois Central Railroad, three miles south of Bradford, has the following business enterprises:
General Merchants.—Powell & Brother, Grant Thetford.
Roller Mills.—Hudson & Thetford.

CADES,

a station on the Illinois Central Railroad, four miles north of Milan, has the following business establishments:
General Traders.—L. G. H. Pittman.
General Merchants.—John Browning.
Sawmills.—William Keton.

EATON.

The village of Eaton, situated in the southwestern portion of the county, on the middle fork of the Forked Deer River, is the oldest town, next to Trenton, in the county. It was a settlement in 1824, and from that time up to the advent of the railroads it was a considerable trading and shipping point. Keel boats were loaded here with the surplus produce of the county, to be transported to the Mississippi River for the New Orleans market. During this period of its history it was a busy place of trade. It is surrounded by a good farming country, but has lagged somewhat in development in recent years. Good land can be bought in the neighborhood of Eaton for from $10 to $20 per acre.

At present the village presents but little evidence of its former importance. A considerable trade is still carried on here.

The business establishments are:
J. W. Smith & Co., a firm composed of J. W. Smith, W. T. Ingram, and B. F. Lemond, general merchants; also operate a sawmill and cotton gin.
General Stores.—C. E. Adams.
Groceries.—A. E. Harbor and A. Dick.

SKETCH OF LIFE OF JUDGE SAMUEL WILLIAMS.

Samuel Williams was born in Smith County, Tenn., July 5, 1815. He was the eldest son of Silas M. Williams. His father moved to Madison County, Tenn., when Samuel was a lad, and settled near the little town of Medon. He was a farmer of small means and Samuel grew up on the farm. About

1835 his father moved to the State of Illinois, where he remained until his death.

His sister, Dicy Williams, married Basil M. Taylor, of Tennessee, in 1837, and she and her husband and Samuel returned to Madison County, Tenn., and Samuel made his home with his brother-in-law for several years. Samuel's education was very limited, as was the case of most of the sons of small farmers of that day. He was often heard to say that he began life for himself by grubbing at $10 per month. During the time he stayed with his brother-in-law he had a lawsuit with a man about a horse trade. He became much interested in the suit and borrowed some law books to investigate the question in the case. He became so fascinated with legal questions that he decided to make a lawyer of himself. Accordingly, he obtained a few law books from Judge John Reed, of Jackson, and read them at night, and at such times as he could spare from his work on the farm. He continued this manner of life for several years, after which he obtained license to practice law. He began the practice of law in Troy, the county seat of Obion County, in 1840. He remained in Troy about five years, and then opened an office in Trenton, Gibson County, having a good practice. He married Miss Katrina M. Walker, of Davidson County, Tenn., on May 6, 1847. In 1858 he was elected Judge of the Circuit Court in the district in which he lived. He remained on the bench until the courts were suspended by the war, in 1862. Owning a large tract of land in Illinois, and the war raging in Tennessee, he moved to Carbondale, Ill., in 1863, and died there on March 3, 1864. Judge Williams left surviving him his wife, who died in 1899, and six children. Matthew, Mercer and Annie have since died. Two of his daughters, Mrs. Sallie Pearce, wife of H. C. Pearce, Esq., and Mrs. Fannie Jelton, wife of J. W. Jelton, reside at Trenton, Tenn., and his son, Rev. S. H. Williams, is now a resident of Newbern, Dyer County, Tenn.

Judge Williams was a consistent member of the Cumberland Presbyterian Church. Although he began life poor, and without influential friends to help him, yet by energy, industry, and sagacity, he made himself an able lawyer and an excellent judge, and accumulated a large estate. His career may be held up as an example to the young men of the country of what a poor boy, without education or influential friends, may make of himself.

But Judge Williams was not an ordinary man. He was richly endowed by nature in many respects. He was energetic, industrious, and had the gift of perseverance, and to these qualities was added a large measure of common sense. As a lawyer, he was a safe counselor; as a judge, he discriminated wisely in the administration of justice. He was eminently practical in everything he undertook, and his broad practical mind illuminated his whole life and crowned it with success. He could not only advise his clients as to their legal rights, but in regard to their business affairs as well, for no subject that was presented seemed to escape the grasp of his uncommon common sense.   J. T. C.

DATES OF ORGANIZATION OF THE COUNTIES OF WEST TENNESSEE.

Shelby	1819
Hardin	1819
Henry	November 7, 1821
Madison	November 7, 1821
Henderson	November 7, 1821
Weakley	November 7, 1821
Carroll	November 11, 1822
McNairy	October 8, 1823
Hardeman	October 10, 1823
Haywood	October 10, 1823
Dyer	October 16, 1823
Gibson	October 21, 1823
Obion	October 24, 1823
Tipton	October 27, 1823
Fayette	September 29, 1824
Lauderdale	November, 1835
Benton	November, 1835
Decatur	November, 1845
Crockett	April, 1872
Lake	June 9, 1870
Chester	1879

If you want cuts or drawings for newspapers, catalogues, programmes, or any kind of stationery, address Southern Advertising and Publishing Company, W. P. Greene, President and Manager, 234 North Market Street, Nashville, Tenn.

ADDENDA.

Persons seeking locations for manufacturing or other business enterprises, or who wish to engage in farming or fruit growing, would do well to address either of the following gentlemen, who will cheerfully furnish any information desired: I. H. Dungan, W. I. McFarland, Humboldt, Tenn.; J. H. Koffman, Fruitland, Tenn.; Albert Biggs, Harry Elder, Trenton, Tenn.; Russell Dance, Dyer, Tenn.; W. P. Elrod, Rutherford, Tenn.; J. W. Howell, Kenton, Tenn.

※ ※

The following lands are advertised for sale by owners:

J. E. Campbell has a body of improved and timbered land in Carroll County, situated about eight miles from the Louisville and Nashville Railroad, twelve miles east of Milan, eight miles south of Trezevant, which is the nearest railroad point. This land is well adapted for farming, well watered by creek and springs. The creek is sufficient to run a water mill. This land may be bought on good terms as a whole or in tracts.

Mr. Campbell also has a fine improved farm of 300 acres ("Oakwood"), good soil, adapted to general farming and stock raising, situated three miles north of Humboldt, which he would part with, as he is devoting himself to other business. Address J. E. Campbell, Humboldt, Tenn.

J. N. Koffman has for sale one good fruit or stock farm, situated on the Humboldt and Gibson Wells road, four miles northwest of Humboldt, Tenn., containing about 47 acres in timber and 120 acres in cultivation. Healthy location. Three settlements and three good tenant houses. One spring of water; good pure well 30 feet deep, also good mineral wells on the farm; as good mineral water as found in this country. Apply to J. N. Koffman, Fruitland, Tenn.

※ ※

ERRATA.

On page 3 of this work, under caption "Regional History," the types put the visit of "Leif the Lucky" to America in the year 1900. This is an arrant falsehood on the part of the type. It should be the year 1000.

※ ※

Illustrations.

The photographic work on this work was done by Mr. Ben Oppenheimer, who did the work for illustrating Trenton; Mr. J. H. Bailey, who did the work for Humboldt; and Mr. Frank Lee, who did the work for Dyer.

※ ※

Some Facts About the United States.

The population of the United States of America in the year 1800 was 5,303,000; in 1900 it was 76,295,220.

The territory of the United States has increased from 1,018,000,000 acres in 1800 to 2,405,000,000 in 1900.

The foreign trade of the United States in 1800 was $162,000,000; now it is $2,244,000,000.

In 1890 the population of Tennessee was 1,767,518; now it is 2,022,723.

If you want an up-to-date job of printing done, address Southern Advertising and Publishing Company, W. P. Greene, President and Manager, 234 North Market Street, Nashville, Tenn.

GENERAL INDEX.

	PAGE.
REGIONAL HISTORY	3
America, Discovery by Columbus	4
America, Discovery by the Cabots	5
America, Early Voyages to	5
America, Naming of	5
America, First English Settlement	6
Charter of King Charles	6
Carolina, North and South	6
Treaty of 1763	8
North Carolina Asserts Sovereignty over Country	8
Treaty of 1788	9
North Carolina Creates Counties	8, 9
Cedes Territory to United States	9
State of Tennessee Admitted	10
Creation of Counties by State	10
Chickasaw Indians	11
Purchase of their Lands	1
Creation of West Tennessee Counties	14, 144
GIBSON COUNTY, ORGANIZATION	12
Col. John H. Gibson	13
First Settlers	14
First Courts	15
Location of County Seat	16
Growth of Population in County	17
Building of the Railroads	18
Description of County	20
County Government	21
Laying Corner Stone of New Courthouse	23
The Judiciary and Bar	26
Religious Interests of County	35
Public Schools	38
Laneview College	40
Medical Society of County	42
County Board of Health	42
Gibson County Fair	42
Gibson County Farmers' Institute	42
West Tennessee Horticultural Society	42
Shorthorn Breeders' Association	42
Assessed Value of Lands	120
Railroad Shipments	121
Transportation Facilities	78
Louisville & Nashville Railroad	78
Mobile & Ohio Railroad	78
Illinois Central Railroad	78
Gibson Wells	78
Masonic Fraternity	79
Taxables of County	81
Old People in County	110
Post Offices in County	132
Addenda	
Errata	

ILLUSTRATIONS AND DESCRIPTIVE ARTICLES.

Jersey Cows, Dr. A. E. Turner's Stock Farm	Cover
Misses Mary and Francis Jarrell	Frontispiece
A First Monday in Trenton	3
Marble Works of James Gillen	5
Some of the Magistrates of County	7
Old Courthouse	18
New Courthouse	23
Magistrates of County	24
Teachers of Gibson County	38
Laneview Assembly Hall	40
Members of Gibson County Medical Society	41
Baptist Church, Humboldt	47
Baptist Church, Trenton	88
Cumberland Presbyterian Church, Humboldt	49
Cumberland Presbyterian Church, Trenton	90
Methodist Church, Humboldt	48
Methodist Church, Trenton	89
Methodist Church, Brazil	133
Presbyterian Church, Trenton	90
Catholic Church, Humboldt	51
Humboldt High School	52
B. C. Jarrell & Co., Factory	64
Dodson Plow Works	65
Cotton Mill, Humboldt	68
Cotton Mill, Trenton	93
Interior of James Gillen's Marble Works, Humboldt	68
Humboldt Spoke Works	69
Beare Bros.' Ice Factory	70
Eclipse Marble Works, Humboldt	71
Merchants' State Bank, Humboldt	72
Bank of Humboldt	73

	PAGE.
Childrens' Playhouse, B. F. Jarrell	75
View of Drug Store of A. Thweatt, Humboldt. Three cuts	76, 77
Some of the Drummers of Gibson County	79
Faculty of Peabody High School	86
Gibson County Bank	91
Interior View of Harrison Dry Goods Company's Store	96
Forked Deer Roller Mill	97
Smith Block, Trenton	100
The Bigelow Hotel	102
T. Harlan & Co., Stave Mill	104
Interior of Mrs. J. G. Sedberry's Millinery Store	105
Interior of J. M. Skiles & Co.'s Store, Trenton	106
Dement Block, Dyer	116
Hearn Block, Dyer	118
Howse & Ragan's Store, Brazil	134

PORTRAITS AND SKETCHES.

Adams, J. J. R.	59
Andrews, Dr. D. T.	142
Andrews, Mrs. D. T.	142
Armstrong, Rev. W. W.	112
Barham, W. C.	131
Bailey, Austin	127
Bailey, George	127
Beucler, Rev. Father	51
Butler, Rev. J. H.	87
Bigelow, John W.	103
Benton, E. E.	105
Campbell, John E.	56
Carthel, Judge John T.	28
Clopton, Dr. R. A.	131
Collinsworth, A. J.	119
Cummins, Prof. J. B.	39
Caldwell, Judge W. C.	28
Collinsworth, Grandfather	83
Cooper, Judge John S.	29
Collinsworth, J. A.	62
Davidson, Miss Essie Mai	124
Dodson, W. H.	66
Dodson, C. J.	67
Dodson, A. R.	62
Dodd, W. H.	80
Dickens, Rev. J. L.	141
Dew, R. J.	32
Dunlap, W. N. L.	56
Dungan, I. H.	61
Elder, John W.	92
Ferrell, Col. C. H.	57
Ferrell, Mrs. C. H.	57
Freed, J.	96
Freeman, Judge Thos. J.	28
Foltz, Frank X.	69
Forrest, Henry N.	107
Garth, Rev. J. G.	51
Gay, Major William	99
Gilbert, Sam	53
Gillespie, J. C.	55
Gillen, James	54
Grizzard, R. E.	98
Gatewood, J. W.	61
Hassell, Prof. A. D.	119
Howell, J. W.	140
Hood, Rev. R. W.	49
Hutchinson, D. J.	31
Hunter, Rev. T. M.	89
Ing, E. W.	71
Ingram, G. W.	34
Jarrell, B. C.	64
Jarrell, Wm.	104
Jewel, Rev. S. L.	88
Jones, Legrand W.	83
Johnson, N. B.	118
Jordan, Rev. W. A.	112
Jetton, Isaac I.	98
Jetton, D. E.	98
Koffman, Dr. J. N.	126
Koffman, J. H.	124
Koffman, Mrs. J. H.	125
Kyzer, J. E.	127
Lannom, J. N.	55
McFarland, W. I.	54
Morgan, L. W.	31
Morgan, R. E.	34
McKee, W. F.	33

GENERAL INDEX, CONTINUED.

	PAGE.
Mathews, Dr. W. F., and family	135
McLeskey, Rev. Joe	50
Neil, Judge M. M.	29
Naylor, Rev. W. J.	89
Oppenheimer, Meyer	94
Oppenheimer, Ben	87
Parr, John Hess	106
Pope, Mrs. Alethia	110
Senter, Neal A.	53
Senter, J. M.	95
Senter, John M.	60
Smith, John R	108
Smith, Leslie W	101
Stallings, J. B.	58
Smith, W. G.	107
Smith, W. L.	100
Stigall, T. M.	74
Stigall, Mrs. T. M.	74
Taylor, R. Z	25
Turner, Dr. A. E.	30
Thompson, J. R.	134
Thweatt, J. J	59
Thweatt, Dr. A.	76
Vick, J. W	109
Wilson, Rev. Lloyd T.	47
Wyatt, H. L.	136
Williamson, Judge John L.	27
Williams, Judge Samuel	27, 143

RESIDENCES.

Adams, J. J. R.	44
Brassfield, Dr. Albert	134
Campbell, J. E.	36
Coley, W. H.	130
Collinsworth, A. J.	83
Deason, J. R.	39
Dunlap, W. N. L.	26
Dodson, A. R.	19
Dement, J. H.	115
Elder, H. M.	11
Foltz, Frank X.	43
Freed, J.	10
Farris, G. W.	113
Ferrell, C. H.	9
Happel, T. J.	14

	PAGE.
Howse, G. R.	19
Jarrell, B. F.	46
Jetton, J. W.	15
Jackson, Dr. J. A.	117
Koffman, Dr. J. N.	126
McDearmon, J. C.	16
Mathews, Dr. W. F.	13
McDaniel, R. B.	114
Mitchell, John B	128
Read, H. C	45
Smith, W. L. (Oak Manor)	86
Senter, John M.	52
Turner, Dr. A. E	138
Wade, W. W.	4
Wade, G. W.	24
Wade, C. R.	130

SPECIAL DESCRIPTIVE ARTICLES.

City of Humboldt	43
City of Trenton	84
City of Dyer	111
Fruitland	123
City of Milan	128
Town of Rutherford	136
Town of Brazil	133
Town of Kenton	138
Village of Medina	141
Village of Bradford	143
Village of Gibson	142
Village of Idlewild	143
Village of Cades	143
Village of Eaton	143
Yorkville and Neighborhood	135
Neboville and Neighborhood	137

ADVERTISEMENTS.

Louisville and Nashville Railroad.
Nashville, Chattanooga and St. Louis Railway.
Mobile and Ohio Railroad.
Illinois Central Railroad.
Saint Louis Coffin Company.
Mayers Chair Company.
Southern Advertising and Publishing Company.
Harrison Dry Goods Company.
Lands for sale.

JERSEY COWS, DR. A. E. TURNER'S STOCK FARM.

www.ingramcontent.com/pod-product-compliance
Lightning Source LLC
Chambersburg PA
CBHW020655300426
44112CB00007B/384